Twenty-Five Years of the Life Review: Theoretical and Practical Considerations

Twenty-Five Years of the Life Review: Theoretical and Practical Considerations

Robert Disch
Editor

Routledge
Taylor & Francis Group
LONDON AND NEW YORK

First published 1988 by The Haworth Press, Inc.

2 Park Square, Milton Park, Abingdon, Oxfordshire OX14 4RN
52 Vanderbilt Avenue, New York, NY 10017

Routledge is an imprint of the Taylor & Francis Group, an informa business

First issued in hardback 2019

LIBRARY OF CONGRESS
Library of Congress Cataloging-in-Publication Data

Twenty-five years of the life review: theoretical and practical considerations / Robert Disch, editor.
p. cm.
"Has also been published as Journal of gerontology social work, volume 12, numbers 3/4, 1988"—T.p. verso.
Includes bibliographies.
ISBN 978-0-866-56836-4 (hbk)
1. Social work with the aged—United States. 2. Gerontology—United States—Biographical methods. 3. Aged—United States—Psychology. I. Disch, Robert. II. Title: 25 years of the life review. III. Title: Life review.
HV 1461. T84 1988
362.6'042—dc 19 88-14703
CIP

ISBN 978-0-86656-836-4 (hbk)

Twenty-Five Years of the Life Review: Theoretical and Practical Considerations

CONTENTS

III. ADAPTATIONS AND APPLICATIONS

ABOUT THE EDITOR

Robert Disch, MA, is Project Director of the Intergenerational Life History Project of the Brookdale Center on Aging of Hunter College in New York City. He is a faculty member and advisory board member of the Institute of Study for Older Adults at New York City Technical College in Brooklyn, as well as a member of the human resources faculty of the College of New Rochelle. He is a contributor to a manual on the methods of organizing and conducting life review projects, and is managing editor of the journal, *Values, Ethics, and Aging: The Journal of Human Values and Aging*.

Preface: "Whom the Gods Would Destroy They First Make Popular"

As readers of this *Journal* are well aware, the concept of the life review as articulated by Dr. Robert Butler in 1963 has become extremely popular both as a theoretical proposition about the nature of the life cycle and as a potent basis for program development with the elderly. Scores of articles have appeared in the professional literature describing and evaluating projects that range from Brownies collecting a few stories at a local senior center to heavy-duty therapy groups in psychiatric institutions. And, as one might have predicted, such rapid success has bred a host of concomitant problems.

In a country where, as a humorist recently put it, even the concept of "crisis" is in crisis, why should the life review receive a different fate? In fact, many indicators suggest that it hasn't. The crisis exists because, as Kathleen Woodward recently observed, "The life review has attained the status of a myth that passes for reality." What forms, we might ask, is this "reality" taking? Here are a few typical events that may help illuminate the nature of the problem:

- A doctoral candidate visits to examine the Brookdale life review projects. He wants to do research on the efficacy of the life review as a tool for enhancing the vitality of long-term marriages;
- The history chair of a large, prestigious New York City high school visits to find out how juniors and seniors can fulfill community service obligations by doing life-review work with neighborhood seniors;

- —A supervisor of five large senior centers calls to inquire if someone can come over to conduct life-history work with her membership. She wants to add this activity to her inventory of recreational programs;
- —The day's mail arrives with two lengthy collections of memoirs done in life review groups. One stresses local history, the other the comings and goings in a senior center. The sender wants to know if Brookdale can arrange to have them published.

Where did these proposals wind up and what do they suggest about the crisis of the life review?

The Doctoral Candidate. Shortly after the visit his advisory committee vetoed the use of the life review as a component in the research design, and rightly so in our opinion. In spite of the good intentions of the student, the imposition of the life review as a "therapy" where none was needed or requested was felt to be unwise at best and potentially harmful at worst. Perhaps a historical analogue is that of the widespread use of X rays to treat benign medical problems—acne, tonsilletis, the common cold—between 1930 and the mid-50s. Since life review partakes of all the characteristics of everyday discourse, it is thought to be relatively benign. A similar argument was made for radiation because X rays occur in nature.

The High School Project. Many high school students now perform community service work to complement their formal studies, but intellectually respectable work roles are hard to find. Hence teachers and administrators are attracted to life review and oral history projects because they appear to be mentally and educationally sound. These programs are preferred to other, less cerebral forms of work with the elderly—like escort service, housecleaning and shopping expeditions. In addition, life review work is thought to have clout with university admissions officers.

What our guests often do not want to hear about is the need to run these programs in an intellectually rigorous manner. In discussion and at workshops, Brookdale trainers stress the desirability of starting small, expanding slowly, organizing efficiently, providing close supervision for teens and elderly, running the project for a minimum of 18 weeks and using experts to instruct the interviewers. The thought of loosing a few hundred ill-equipped teenagers on the community elderly because the life review is perceived as a "good thing" is highly undesirable. Ironically, it is the very attractiveness and potency of the life review that leads to grandiose thinking.

The Bandwagon Syndrome. Another manifestation of the problem is the felt necessity on the part of many center directors and recreation specialists to start life review programs for their clientele. And that is as it should be. If life review is everything that the literature claims it to be, could these professionals do anything else? Certainly, few who have conscientiously worked with Butler's theory would want to withold it from any group of seniors. But there are too many instances where the bandwagon syndrome leads to such low quality work that it would be better if these programs never started. As in the case of the high school program, we advise careful planning, small groups, and good project design. If such cannot be obtained, it's better to wait and not "pollute the well" with a second-rate program that will turn people off.

Poorly run programs always leave a bitter aftertaste and a population who will be reluctant to participate if the opportunity later arises to join a quality project, as often happens. Once again, the very success of the life review can lead to problems.

Publish or Perish. In the fourth instance, one that reflects the desire to publish everything that is uttered by anyone over the age of 65, we uncover instances of acute condescension. The content of what is collected in the course of life history work ranges from utterly fascinating to irredeemably uninteresting beyond the immediate context of the interviewer and the interviewee. Over the transom manuscripts may contain interesting sections, but they also contain sentences like, "In the afternoon it started to rain. Dad went to the Center for his pool game and Mother followed later on . . . It made for a long, full day . . . The days went by one after the other. . . . " And so on. In such cases a compromise is usually suggested. We recommend that the manuscript be copied on acid-free paper and donated to the local library and/or historical society. That way the worthwhile material will be saved for future generations.

Similar problems appear in creative writing, arts and crafts, dramatic productions and in any program where overzealous instructors exchange honesty for the kinds of condescension that contribute to short term gains in group functioning or ego building.

Life review is not alone as an area of interest threatened by success. In 1970 Professor Rudolph J. Vecolli, the historian of immigration, complained bitterly that his field was being slighted in the research and writing about America. In 1979 he wrote an article in which he argued that the sudden popularization of immigration studies was lowering standards and undermining scholarship, that what was needed was a period of benign neglect! The evidence strongly suggests that a similar development has taken place in the domain of the life review.

It was a perception of these and other concerns that influenced the editor in the selection of articles for this issue. Taken as a whole the essays constitute a kind of dialectic about the life review and an effort to go beyond Butler's early formulation both in theory and practice. In the first half of the volume some of the essays deal with ways in which the theory is being questioned, modified and expanded. Pertinent here are the essays by Moody, Woodward, Kivnick and Weingarten. In the second half, the essays show some exemplary ways in which these criticisms can be adapted to practical purposes. The essays by Doris Francis on art and Susan Perlstein on drama, in particular, take off from the autobiographical beginnings so graphically described by Marc Kaminsky in his exploration of a life review group in the South Bronx. For these authors, as for the West German psychologist, Peter Sprinkart, the various adaptations of the life review can be a liberating, empowering experience when done in the right way.

Robert Disch

I. INTRODUCTION

Twenty-Five Years of the Life Review: Where Did We Come From? Where Are We Going?

Harry R. Moody

When I was a small boy, my grandfather often used to take me alone for walks to places in our town I had never been before. On those trips Grandpa never said very much about himself or his life, although I was always very curious about him and eager to learn about the years when he had grown up. But he died in 1958, long before the idea of life review became popular, and so I never heard from him the stories I had waited as a child to hear.

By contrast, my Aunt Mabel, nearly Grandpa's age, was of an entirely different sort. She was a born talker, about herself mostly, and she went on like six characters in search of an author, endlessly recounting tales of bygone days. On each visit to see her, as we gathered around to listen to her nonstop reminiscences, I would always impatiently await the time when our visit would be over and I could gain the merciful respite of living in the present. By the time she finally died, her reveries of the past had entirely swallowed up the present.

I never got to hear my grandfather's reminiscences, so today I can imagine his stories to be anything I want them to be. That imaginary version of his stories is more satisfying than Aunt Mabel's

---

Harry R. Moody is Deputy Director of the Brookdale Center on Aging of Hunter College. His publications include many articles on the humanities and aging, as well as the forthcoming book, *The Abundance of Life: Human Development Policies for an Aging Society*, to be published by the Columbia University Press in 1988.

stories actually proved to be in fact. But then that is the way it is with imaginary tales. The imagination works to fill in the empty spaces with our hopes or fears. I sometimes wonder what would have become of either Aunt Mabel or Grandpa if in their old age they had been enrolled as members of groups devoted to a program of reminiscence and life review, those groups found today in so many senior centers or nursing homes. Would that formal reminiscence induced by professional intervention have made the outcome any different from the "natural" result that became a part of my own childhood memories?

WHY DO WE CARE ABOUT LIFE REVIEW?

We may ask the further question: Why we care so much about life review or reminiscence at all? Professionals in gerontology will answer that they promote and encourage reminiscence because they believe it is, somehow, a "good thing," whether for the old people who tell the stories or the children who use them to fill up the empty spaces in the imagination. There is something to this idea of reminiscence and life review that is compelling, something which is very far from being merely a form of group-work or a technique of therapy. The idea of life review is, finally, more akin to a wish, a hope, an act of the imagination itself. So the professional enthusiasm for reminiscence and oral history and other life history methods is quite understandable. Whether natural or unnatural, we care about it for reasons we find hard to express because they reflect our deepest hopes and fears. Is reminiscence an activity somehow induced because we, the young ones, fear to find nothing more in that empty space of old age beyond an imaginary story, a story that was never told, a silence that frightens us as an anticipation of our own old age?

In a very brief time, barely twenty-five years, the concept of life review as a rationale for reminiscence in old age has earned a well-established place in the theory and practice of gerontology. Precisely because life history activities are now subject to professional control and theoretical validation, we are entitled to ask: Are life history activities among old people really a "natural" process, perhaps with an evolutionary basis[1] or are they an artificial product shaped by social interventions of questioning and listening on the part of professionals who organize and manage life history activities? Does life review have adaptational significance—for example, on depression and mental health? Does it have no effect, or do the effects go in the opposite direction?[2] Is the transmission of life history a desirable activity to encourage among the old or does it represent a distraction, an evasion or even a negative activity? Opinions on all these questions have divided sharply over the last quarter century.[3]

On the one hand, many gerontologists and practitioners have tended to see life history as a natural impulse of old age. Where Aristotle viewed the reminiscence of the old as a sign of failing mental powers, modern gerontologists have looked to reminiscence as an opportunity for personal integration, psychological healing, and self-actualization, all now seen as a natural potential of late life development. The motif of redemption through recovery of past time originated with the Romantic poets, especially Wordsworth (*The Prelude*). In due course it achieved supreme expression in Proust's great novel *Remembrance of Things Past*. Who has not heard of the teacup scene where the narrator, Marcel, recovers the long-lost memory of childhood innocence as he encounters sensations of taste that plunge him back to a world long forgotten? The French title of Proust's work is actually better translated as "in search of time lost," and today that search still goes on. It is nowhere more evident than in the psychology of old age.

This motif of redemption through autobiographical memory is an indispensable ingredient in a whole genre of films about old age. I have in mind a genre that reaches from Bergman's *Wild Strawberries* right up to the recent film *The Trip to Bountiful*, both films where the hero or heroine journeys back to places of lost childhood and, at the end of life, comes full circle to find "lost time" and the lost self. Films of this genre, like earlier poems and novels, reinforce a hopeful picture of the last stage of life, a time when autobiographical memory—in short, life review—might allow us one last chance to find meaning in life. It is not an accident that Erik Erikson, perhaps the greatest fashioner of a "psychological mythology" of the stages of life, would devote a brilliant essay to showing how scenes in *Wild Strawberries* exhibit the achievement of insight and "ego integrity" as the hero struggles to recover and master the unresolved conflicts of time lost.[4] If *Wild Strawberries* unfolds a "Proustian" aesthetic, then the psychology of ego integrity and life review together comprise a collective myth that inspires a hopeful view of old age and its possibilities.

In light of this powerful and positive cultural myth of late-life reminiscence, it is not surprising that gerontologists should take a vigorous interest in late-life memory and its possibilities for personal renewal.[5] If the claims of life-review are upheld, then might we not find a *natural* basis for the spiritual impulses expressed so movingly in poetry, fiction and film? This claim that life review is a natural or "spontaneously occurring" tendency was in fact one of Robert Butler's main reasons for insisting that gerontologists should take the phenomenon of reminiscence more seriously.[6] And Butler's advice was dutifully followed. In the years since his seminal article first appeared, gerontologists have increasingly looked with favor on all sorts of life history activities, seeing in them an appropriate means of promoting the life review along with all the other virtues that are supposed to accompany it.[7]

Skeptics, on the other hand, have taken a different view. They have tended to see life history methods as far from "natural," and indeed as just one more unproven intervention or, still worse, as an imposition by professionals intent on imposing their own image of late life development. In the first place, there are the skeptics, the empiricists, the investigators who looked at reminiscence groups and found no gains in mental health, indeed sometimes even found losses—depression—as a result of engaging in life review. If reminiscence is seen as a technique, an instrument for achieving a specific goal, then it inevitably opens itself up to this kind of empirical confirmation or refutation.[8]

Philosophical critics, like Simone de Beauvoir, have taken an entirely different point of view.[9] Beauvoir and others reject the entire framework of psychological integration promised by life review and would urge a very different form of self-fulfillment in the last stage of life. Far from seeing life review as a natural phenomenon of late life, these critics have seen it, at worst, as a betrayal of what the challenge of old age really presents us with. Instead of turning inward or looking toward the past, we are urged to turn outward and to live in the present, for an activist old age. In this view, the notion that life review is somehow "natural" then becomes simply an evasion of the human challenge to make our lives, and old age not least, whatever we can make of them.

LIFE REVIEW IN HISTORICAL CONTEXT

The notion that life review is a "natural" process, then, remains a controversial point. But one point that cannot be denied is that, in our own recent history, there was a time when life review and reminiscence were *not* held in high esteem at all. Practitioners active in the 1950s remember well that in those years there was no special encouragement to find meaning in the recollections of old people. What happened? What changed and why?

The usual answer, often only implicit, is that in "the bad old days" before life review and reminiscence were "discovered," gerontological practitioners ignored or discounted the phenomenon. On this view of the matter, we now live in an enlightened time and we have "discovered" (not invented) the process of life review as part of a more general affirmation of the positive psychology of late life. A very similar account, incidentally, could be given if we were telling the story of the "discovery" of oral history and the way in which oral history has been tied to the recovery and validation of the lives of ordinary people and, in particular, the lives of groups, such as women or minorities, disregarded by historians of the past. The point here is simply that the validation of life history methods *itself* has a history. The way that we see that history depends on the kind of narrative we want to offer for our own recent past, including our own narrative about the history of old age and the history of groups bypassed by the "grand narratives" of political history in the past.[10]

The "discovery" of life review is, finally, part of a "progressive" view of history—the present is better than the past, we know more today than they knew then. It amounts to saying that, in the "bad old days" the elderly and their life experiences were simply disregarded but now we know better. Discoveries were made and progress has taken place. This progressive view of history makes the popularity of life history methods in the field of aging quite understandable. But the progressive view also resembles, in disturbing ways, what Butterfield satirized as the "Whig View of History" (the idea that past historical change in unenlightened epochs was a natural preparation for the later triumph of science, reason, and law). As far as life history methods are concerned this progressive view is tied to an assumption that life review is *both* a "natural" process *and also* one offering a kind of liberation or breakthrough into the fullness that is possible only when we recover the lost past.

But this resolution of contradictions is more apparent than real. As soon as we look beneath the surface, we encounter disturbing questions that proponents of life history methods must be prepared to answer. Those questions are worth asking because, if our social interventions serve to shape, in subtle ways, the process and outcome of life history activities, then we are obliged to examine far more critically the underlying values and presuppositions that make us to look so favorably on life history activity among old people. Without that critical examination, life history activities run the risk of reifying and mystifying our individual and collective cultural or historical experience.

Life history activities retain their overwhelming power and attractiveness for us not because they are scientifically validated means of professional practice but because life history activities evoke our most deeply held hopes and wishes about what the last stage of life should be. Those hopes are just that: not "facts," but a kind of myth or collective wish-fulfillment intent on transforming old age in modern society and, ultimately, offering an alternative sense of meaning in a world where the last stage of life tends to be drained of meaning altogether. This does not mean that life review is to be rejected or even demythologized. But if I am correct in my suspicion that life review is a new kind of gerontological myth, then it deserves the most searching scrutiny. Without critical attention, the practice of life review is in danger of becoming a kind of ersatz religion into which we unwittingly project conflicting hopes and wishes about the end of life. All these hopes and wishes stubbornly resist empirical refutation and rational codification into technical or instrumental forms. But they resist codification for reasons that have nothing to do with the success or failure of particular intervention designs. At bottom, our hopes and wishes about life history activities in old age express a shared cultural ambivalence toward the remembered past itself, toward the meaning of old age, and, not least, toward death.[11]

THE PURPOSE OF LIFE-HISTORY METHODS

A review of the gerontological literature over the last quarter century will confirm that gerontological professionals of many backgrounds have held a laudatory opinion of life history activities. Since Robert Butler first proposed life review as an interpretation of reminiscence in old age, professionals have seen life history activities as something to be encouraged and managed for noble social purposes. These purposes have included oral history research, intergenerational transmission, and therapeutic intervention on behalf of the mental health of the elderly. The justification of reminiscence in terms of all three goals—historical, educational, or therapeutic—has been proclaimed repeatedly in the literature of gerontology. But the goals themselves, and the relation between goals and practice, ends and means, have largely been taken for the granted. In keeping with the scientific and professional ethos of gerontology, investigators have posed their questions in narrow terms as they looked for techniques or methods that would permit professionals to achieve those goals and, at the same time, legitimize gerontology as a discipline with some claim to scientific or professional status.

We can group the purposes of life history with the aging into three broad categories: the therapeutic, the cultural, and the historical-political.

Gerontologists who adopt a therapeutic agenda have dominated the literature on the subject of life review from its inception. They have typically come from the health professions (psychiatry, social work, or nursing) and in all these fields, there is a substantial literature on the therapeutic uses of life review with the elderly.[12] Even oral history has been justified in therapeutic terms.[13] According to the therapeutic point of view, the working assumption is that life history activities help old people attain the psychological integration promised by the Romantic myth extending from Wordsworth to Proust and beyond. But now, we are told, instead of merely an aesthetic image of wholeness, therapeutic life history methods hold out a scientifically validated technique for accomplishing the goal of fulfillment in old age. To understand the power of this therapeutic agenda, we must understand the nature of therapeutic culture itself.

Philip Rieff defines our "therapeutic culture" in these terms: "Our cultural revolution does not aim, like its predecessors, at victory for some rival commitment, but rather at a way of using all commitments, which amounts to loyalty toward none."[14] What "the triumph of the therapeutic" means is that, by psychologizing about ourselves interminably, we transcend good and evil, truth and falsehood, in favor of a new "therapeutic imperative," where "nothing [is] at stake beyond a manipulatable sense of well-being."[15] The rise of a therapeutic culture, symbolized by the power of the mental health industry, signifies a shift from a controlling to a releasing concept of culture, away from restrictive morality and toward antinomian ideals of self-expression, tied to an infinite variety of impulse needs.

How are we to understand the fate of life review in such a therapeutic culture? One way is to see the lapse of old-fashioned standards (sin, guilt, remorse, etc.) in favor of the autobiographical consciousness itself: the endless quest for ever new "metaphors of self," to employ the term used by Olney in his important study of literary autobiography.[16] In fact, modern autobiography originated in a religious sensibility exemplified by works like Augustine's *Confessions* or John Bunyan's *Autobiography*, products of a moralizing culture. But modern therapeutic culture does not understand autobiography in these objective religious categories at all. Rather, as Olney describes it, modern autobiography is a kind of mythmaking, the creation of endless alternative perspectives (fictions, metaphors) on the self: in short, a prefabricated past.[17] Both autobiography and life review become equivalent to the search for a life myth, but an infinitely manipulatable myth which can be judged only in terms of whether it is "functional" in mental health terms: for example, whether or not it leads to "life satisfaction" or "successful aging."[18]

The second powerful use of life history methods with the aged is for purpose of cultural transmission: passing on the values or lessons of the past to succeeding generations.[19] Two of the best examples of this are the work of Barbara Myerhoff and the series of books published by Elliot Wigginton describing the Foxfire phenomenon.[20] Myerhoff's book, *Number Our Days* along with the Emmy Award-winning film of the same name, won acclaim because the story told by Myerhoff was, finally, the story of the Prodigal Daughter returning to rediscover her roots by recording the stories of the Old Ones.[21] The Foxfire project began as a program for high school students to learn about the vanished folklore of rural elders. It has gone on to become a publishing phenomenon, a Broadway play, and a national foundation promoting intergenerational transmission between old and young. Many other intergenerational programs flourish in America today because they evidently respond to a deeply felt need to devise new forms of generational continuity.

If the therapeutic use of life history aims at creating a personal sense of meaning, then the cultural use of life history aims at creating collective forms of meaning—recreating old myths that celebrate vanished communities, whether the East European Jewish Shtetl or the Little House on the Prairie. In this process of cultural transmission, the old ones are cast in the role of vital links in the chain of generations. Instead of being bypassed or cast aside, as the grand narrative of Progress might imply, the old are thrust again into center stage. If the young no longer understand or respect the "world of our fathers," it is because they have not heard the stories that would make that world come alive. But it is obvious that this condition of generational discontinuity is one of the unavoidable conditions of modern life.[22] In these circumstances the intergenerational agenda for life history work with the old easily becomes an exercise in nostalgia. Like antique furniture, the lived memories of the past now take on great value but precisely because they are no longer useful except as objects to inspire us. Like the golden bird in Yeats' poem "Sailing to Byzantium," the tales of the old ones serve to distract the young "from what is past, or passing, or to come." But these tales no longer exist in historical time which binds past, present, and future together.

It is the last purpose of life history methods, the investigatory technique of oral history, that promises to confront historical time in the most direct fashion. Here we must distinguish between oral history as a method of scholarly inquiry as opposed to oral history in a wider political or ideological sense. Historian Alan Nevins created the Oral History Archive at Columbia University essentially to insure access to a unique source of data (oral testimony) for understanding our recent past.[23] The agenda of popular writers on oral history has been quite different. When Alex Haley wrote *Roots* or Studs Terkel wrote *Working* or *The Good War*, they were engaged in a social or political agenda. The same point holds true for documentary film-makers: for example, European film-makers in works like *The Sorrow and the Pity* or *Shoah* who have used oral history techniques to recover the experience of the Nazi Occupation and the Holocaust. For popular oral historians the memories of old people are not simply access to a lost past but a promise of new ways of thinking about the present or creating a better world in the future.

In fact, the line between popular and academic oral history is not nearly so firm as one might imagine. Among academic historians the renewed respectability of oral history in the last two decades has gone hand in hand with the rise of the "new social history" (now of course not so new) which has helped validate the life experience of groups bypassed or overlooked by traditional histories.[24] In short, "bottom-up history," including oral history as one of its techniques, has offered an alternative narrative and a challenge to many of the grand narratives embodied in our collective picture of the past, including those narratives of progress which suppressed the experience of groups whose voices were not heard by official versions of the past.

This conception of oral history, whether popular or academic, has clear implications for the use of life history methods with older people. In the first place, the line between public and private history is eroded: private experience (sexuality, family life) suddenly becomes part of the public agenda. Second, those groups whose experience has been marginalized by the dominant society now acquire a voice and an acknowledgement of their point of view. Third, the position of the elderly, themselves often marginalized, itself begins to change. As the "grand narratives" lose legitimacy, alternative narratives are considered, and one of these alternatives is a new story of old age itself. Oral history on its face vindicates the importance of the life experience of old people, which is no longer simply obsolete, as it is under conditions of modernization. Under an alternative narrative, the elderly, as repositories of living memories, now become resources for social change, for making a better world. When life history is conceived as a form of intergenerational transmission, then the young are reminded to look to the models of the past and the old are cast in the role of custodians of that past. When life history is conceived of as oral history with a political agenda, then the old are cast in the role of actors who will help shape the future.

CONCLUSION: TWO CHEERS FOR LIFE REVIEW

I have argued here that life review has achieved the prominence it has in the last generation because it serves, in effect, as a new kind of gerontological myth. The danger of this myth is that we uncritically project into it all the hopes and wishes about what the last stage of life should be.[25] Now there is nothing wrong with having hopes and wishes, and there is nothing wrong with the broad purposes to which life history methods have been put: namely, the purposes of therapy, intergenerational transmission, and political struggle. On the contrary, all have validity.

Unlike the empiricists, I would not argue that life review, as a mythic category, should be judged by strictly scientific or instrumental tools of verification. The purpose of life history methods is far broader than what our tools are likely to capture. The danger is they we may cut the activities down to the size that our tools can measure. Unlike Simone de Beauvoir and other "activist" critics, I would not agree that the activity of memory and imagination, consciousness and communication, is devoid of meaning unless it is tied to direct activity in the world. On the contrary, to deprive the elderly of an important role in these activities—of myth, memory, and imagination—is, in the end, to deprive society of the gifts that can be acquired and perfected by that group of people, the old ones, who have gained something from their life experience and now have the leisure, even the compulsion, to appraise the meaning of that long life experience. Simone de Beauvoir, after all, herself wrote four lengthy volumes of her own autobiography, and writing, like speaking, is as much a form of activity as anything is. What prompts the activity is the search for meaning, individual or collective.[26]

But life review, and life history methods, by themselves, cannot bear the full weight of that search for meaning. We do not find "meaning" inside our own heads. We need to have a more modest attitude toward life review, not to see in it an ersatz religion but simply as one method for engaging older people with whatever sources of renewal do provide meaning in life: from family and community to religion and the historical or political order. By living beyond themselves, in a world order that gives intelligibility to the individual life, people discover meaning. In so doing, the objective world order and the individual self are bound together. But that task is no easy thing to achieve, in late life or at any time of life.

The achievement is not made any easier in a therapeutic culture. Instead of accepting the "triumph of the therapeutic" in understanding old age reminiscence, we should be more open to *objective* sources of meaning—that is, sources of meaning beyond the individual self. Among other things this means demystifying the professional-technical categories of explanation that have dominated discussion of life review since its beginning. Instead of technical explanation, we need a phenomenological approach to life history work.[27] Instead of the categories of psychotherapy alone, we need the categories of literature, of religion, and of politics for a full account of the narratives of old people.[28]

Above all, we need to remember that life history methods, whether understood as therapy, as intergenerational transmission, or as oral history, are always *social*.[29] This means appreciating how the life story is told depends in crucial ways on the listener, the audience. Listeners are not simply passive transcribers or detached professionals because our social interventions are always shaping the stories we hear. The listener and speaker, finally, are both co-creators of the story.[30] We fill in the empty spaces by an act of imagination that converts silence into speech. Once we see that empty space for what it is, we need no longer fear it.

At the end of his life Gauguin painted a vast, magnificent canvas that hangs today in the Boston Museum of Fine Arts. From that painting haunting faces stare out across the empty space of the vault and ask an insistent question. The painting bears the title: "Who are we? Where did we come from? Where are we going?" Life review asks that question as insistently as those faces do, and answering it is a monumental task. We can only acknowledge this monumental task for what it is if we keep the questions alive. Twenty-five years after the concept of life review was introduced, the questions are as alive as ever.

REFERENCE NOTES

1. N. Mergler and M. Goldstein, "Why There Are Old People: Senescence as Biological & Cultural Preparedness for the Transmission of Information," *Human Development* (1983), 26: 72-90.

2. A. McMahon and Paul Rhudick, "Reminiscing: Adaptational Significance in the Aged," *Archives of General Psychiatry* (Mar., 1964); P. Perrotta and J.A. Meacham, "Can A Reminiscing Intervention Alter Depression & Self-Esteem?" *International Journal of Aging & Human Development*, 1981-2 14(1), 23-30; P. Brennan and L.D. Steinberg, "Is Reminiscence Adaptive?" *International Journal of Aging & Human Development*, (1983-84), 18:1, 99-110.

3. Harry R. Moody, "A Bibliography on Reminiscence and Life Review," in M. Kaminsky (ed.), *Uses of Reminiscence*, 1984; V. Molinari and R.E. Reichlin, "Life Review Reminiscence in the Elderly: A Review of the Literature," *International Journal of Aging & Human Development*, (1985), 20: 81-92.

4. Erik Erikson, "Reflections on Dr. Borg's Life Cycle," *Daedelus*, 1968; Erik Erikson, *Life History and the Historical Moment*, New York: Norton, 1975.

5. Marc Kaminsky, *The Uses of Reminiscence*, New York: The Haworth Press, 1984.

6. Robert Butler, "The Life Review: An Interpretation of Reminiscence in the Aged," *Psychiatry*, Vol. 26, 1963.

7. Robert Butler, "The Life Review: An Unrecognized Bonanza," *International Journal of Aging & Human Development*, 12(1) (1980-81).

8. Michael & Jean Romaniuk, "Looking Back: An Analysis of Reminiscence Functions and Triggers," *Experimental Aging Research*, 7 (1981), 477-489.

9. Simone de Beauvoir, *The Coming of Age* (trans. Patrick O'Brian), New York: 1972.

10. Quinton Skinner (ed.), *The Return of Grand Theory in the Human Sciences*, New York: Cambridge University Press, 1985.

11. Ernest Becker, *The Denial of Death*, New York: The Free Press, 1973.

12. J. Linton and S.C. Olstein, "Therapeutic Aspects of Reminiscence," *Social Casework*, 50 (1969), 263-268; M.L. Gerfo, "Three Ways of Reminiscence in Theory and Practice," *International Journal of Aging & Human Development*, 12 (1980/81), 39-48; Pamela Babb de Ramon, "The Final Task: Life Review for

the Dying Patient," *Nursing*, 13:2 (February, 1983); M.R. Wysocki, "Life Review for the Elderly Patient," *Nursing* (February, 1983), 13(2); K.S. King, "Reminiscing Psychotherapy with Aging People," *Psychosocial Nursing and Mental Health Services*, (February, 1983), 21-25; Elizabeth Williams, "Building Tales," *Activities, Adaptation & Aging* (1983), 4(1): 63-69.

13. Willa Baum, "The Therapeutic Value of Oral History," *International Journal of Aging & Human Development*, 12(1) (1980-81); Raymond Harris and S. Harris, "Therapeutic Uses of Oral History Techniques in Medicine," *International Journal of Aging & Human Development*, 12(1) (1980-81).

14. Philip Rieff, *The Triumph of the Therapeutic: Uses of Faith After Freud*, New York: Harper, 1968, p. 21.

15. *Ibid.*, p. 13.

16. James Olney, *Metaphors of Self: The Meaning of Autobiography*, Princeton, NJ: Princeton University Press, 1980.

17. Peter L. Berger, "Excursus: Alternation & Biography: Or: How to Acquire a Prefabricated Past," in *Invitation to Sociology*, Garden City, NY: Anchor-Doubleday, 1963, pp. 54-65.

18. Robert Butler, "Successful Aging & the Role of the Life Review," in S.H. Zarit, *Readings in Aging & Death*, 1977.

19. Tamara Hareven, "The Search for Generational Memory: Tribal Rites in Industrial Society," *Daedalus* (Fall, 1978), Vol. 107, No. 4.

20. Eliot Wigginton (ed.), *The Foxfire Book*, Garden City, NY: Anchor-Doubleday, 1972 (1973, 1975, 1977).

21. Barbara Myerhoff, *Number Our Days*, New York: Dutton, 1979.

22. Ronald Blythe, *The View in Winter: Reflections on Old Age*, New York: Penguin, 1979; Marshall Berman, *All That Is Solid Melts into Air*, New York: Simon and Schuster, 1982.

23. Glenn H. Elder, *Children of the Great Depression: Social Change in Life Experience*, Chicago: University of Chicago Press, 1974; Paul Thompson, *The Voice of the Past: Oral History*, New York: Oxford University Press, 1978.

24. Susan Benson and Stephen Brier, *Presenting the Past*, Philadelphia: Temple University Press, 1986.

25. Harry R. Moody, "The Meaning of Life and the Meaning of Old Age," in T. Cole and S. Gadow (eds.), *What Does It Mean to Grow Old? Views from the Humanities*, Durham, NC: Duke University Press, 1986.

26. Barbara Myerhoff, "Re-membered Lives," *Parabola: Myth & the Quest for Meaning* 5(1), (1980) pp. 22-40.

27. Jerold M. Starr, "Toward a Social Phenomenology of Aging: Studying the Self Process in Biographical Work," *Aging & Human Development* (1982-83), 16:4, 255-270.

28. Mark Freeman, "History, Narrative and Life-Span Developmental Knowledge," *Human Development* (1984), 27: 1-19; Kenneth Gergen & M. Gergen, "Narrative form and the Construction of Psychological Theory," in T.R. Sarbin (ed.) *The Narrative Perspective in Psychology*, New York: Praeger.

29. Debra David, *The Uses of Memory: Social Aspects of Reminiscence in Old Age*, (Dissertation), U. of California, Berkeley, 1981: Harry R. Moody, "Reminiscence and the Recovery of the Public World," in Kaminsky, *Uses of Reminiscence*, 1984.

30. Barbara Myerhoff, "Life History Among the Elderly: Performance, Visibility, & Re-Membering," in Kurt Back (ed.), *Life Course: Integrative Theories and Exemplary Populations*, Boulder, CO: Westview Press, 1980.

II. THEORY AND INTERPRETATION

Reminiscence, Identity, Sentimentality: Simone de Beauvoir and the Life Review

Kathleen Woodward

I

The decade of the seventies in the United States witnessed the rise of oral history, a new methodology in historical studies. Implicit in that method—fittingly so for many researchers who had been students during the radical sixties—was a concern for the dispossessed. Many younger historians turned from political and economic history to study social history and the experiential dimensions of everyday life. Interestingly enough, the impulse was both liberal and conservative at the same time. Accompanying the agenda to constitute a new canon by writing the histories of groups of people who had been excluded from the master narratives (histories of women are perhaps the best example) was also the effort to preserve and conserve and—in its sentimental extreme—to hallow.

If in the seventies the life stories of members of various underclasses, subcultures, and racial and artistic minorities were captured on tape for the record, no group was regarded with such sentimentality as the elderly. One brief anecdotal example will, I hope, suffice. At a conference on gerontology and the humanities in Missouri in 1980 I vividly remember an articulate historian in his mid-thirties who presented the life stories he had collected of elderly people with an effusion so excessive it could best be explained by his weak-

---

Kathleen Woodward is Director of the Center for Twentieth Century Studies and Associate Professor of English at the University of Wisconsin—Milwaukee. Her many publications include *At Last, the Real Distinguished Thing: The Late Poems of Eliot, Pound, Stevens and Williams* and the recent *Memory and Desire: Aging-Literature-Psychoanalysis* (co-edited with Murray M. Schwartz).

ness for any story told by people sixty-five or older. He praised the wisdom of their insights (which in fact were for the most part banal) and the style of their narration (which was most often dull and conventional). As if a pious son he proudly showed us their photographs, remarking on their vitality, as in this case: "Here's Emma. Can you guess how old she is? She's seventy-six and doesn't look a day over sixty-five!" Significantly, here his blind admiration moved beyond the bounds of reverse ageism—his belief that any life story produced by someone over sixty-five is worthy of our reverence—to reveal its opposite: his unexamined moral was that the older she was and the younger she looked, the better—that is, that old age is best when its wears the guise of youth. His mawkishness, in other words, was coupled with an attitude of unconscious superiority and paternalism. Few researchers, of course, have the analytic and literary gifts of the psychologist Robert Coles whose sensitive and deft little book *The Old Ones of New Mexico*, which appeared in 1975, is in my judgment a model of oral history.[1] But even that little book, so expertly shaped, many readers have found cloying in its tribute to a kind of wisdom that came in old age to the Mexican-Americans who were the object of his study.

In retrospect it seems no coincidence that the psychiatrist Robert Butler's article "The Life Review: An Interpretation of Reminiscence in the Aged" should have appeared in the sixties.[2] In that seminal piece Butler argues for the uses of remembrance in the elderly from a psychological point of view. In a gesture analogous to that of the social historians I have been invoking, he theorized that in old age individuals expand their personal histories to include what has been forgotten, perhaps repressed; in so doing, the old (or those younger who are near death) have the opportunity to see their lives whole as in a narrative and—in an Eriksonian formulation—to accept or reject the narratives they have made of their lives. From this point of view we can understand Butler's theory of the life review as a liberal politics of the psyche. In the sixties it helped rescue reminiscence in the elderly from the contempt in which it had been held, scorned as a sign of an infantile return to the past. For Butler such reminiscence was not a symptom of degeneration but rather the mark of a normative process that can serve the process of psychological integration.

Elsewhere I have considered Butler's theory of the life review at some length, arguing among other things that his notion of what constitutes a narrative is neither sufficiently psychoanalytic or literary.[3] Before turning to Simone de Beauvoir, whose work both parallels and diverges from Butler's in interesting ways, I want to note in a Foucauldian vein that Butler's essay—the *knowledge* it has produced—has had a remarkable influence—that is, *power*—in a wide range of spheres extending from social work and nursing to theater and literature. As we know, over the years the notion of the life review has passed beyond the barrier of the technical vocabulary of psychiatric geriatrics. One of the effects of its popular currency is that it has been much debased. At the same time it has been institutionalized and professionalized. Academic conferences are devoted to the life review, and personnel in the United States and abroad are trained in the techniques of aiding—and abetting—old people to do the work of reviewing their lives. A recent case in point is London's Age Exchange theater company which bases its theater pieces on the taped reminiscences of elderly people. In the hands of Age Exchange the life review is understood not as a complex psychological process in the individual which can bring pain as well as a measure of understanding but as a group process that is, in the words of the artistic director, therapeutic in a "sympathetic way" and "pleasurable in a celebratory way." One of the risks of this, of course, is that controlled group reminiscing can itself produce stereotypes ("That was my life in a nutshell," said one elderly man after seeing one of their productions) and devolve into mere entertainment ("So much better than the telly," said another). Another is sheer commercialization (Age Exchange plans, for example, to establish in the near future a "reminiscence center" which, among other things, will sell copies of the transcripts of the tapes they have already recorded).[4]

It would be fair to conclude, I think, that like the work of Age Exchange theater (whose sincerity I do not doubt), on the whole the books which basically take the life review as subject and method and have been successful in the United States in the seventies—books such as the late Barbara Myerhoff's *Number Our Days* or Kenneth Koch's *I Never Told Anybody: Teaching Poetry Writing in a Nursing Home*[5]—are celebratory in nature, written in praise of the elderly by those younger. The sharp cutting edge of Butler's theory of the life review—with its emphasis on guilt and depression as well as wisdom—has been significantly dulled. Here we might speculate that recording the life reviews of other people can perform the function of a kind of surrogate inverse of the life review in one's middle years, the projection of one's life (that is, one's old age) into future time as a way of constructing one's future identity through the experiences of others. If this is indeed the case, it would make sense that the dominant impulse should be celebratory for do we not hope for a satisfactory old age for ourselves?

While in the United States Butler was both making the case for reminiscence in old age and challenging the dispossession of the elderly in American society (we recall that his 1975 book *Why Survive? Being Old in America* won a well-deserved Pulitzer Prize[6]), in France the influential intellectual and writer Simone de Beauvoir was also writing about the devaluation of the elderly in the West. Like Butler's *Why Survive, La Vieillesse*[7] (published in France in 1970) is a volume of compendious research and an expose of the dismaying treatment of the elderly in contemporary society. It represents a prodigious effort to explore the roots of ageism from social, economic, and psychological perspectives. But unlike Butler's sobering manifesto, *La Vieillesse* was written out of personal experience: as a woman of sixty when *La Vieillesse* was published, Beauvoir felt herself to be at the crossroads of a definitive old age. We have every reason to expect, then, that *La Vieillesse* would have received favorable attention if not acclaim in the United States when it appeared in translation in 1972. Yet quite the opposite was in fact the case. The book was published, tellingly, under the ambiguous if not completely misleading title *The Coming of Age* as if to obscure its real subject—old age. It met with a wave of censure by journalists and gerontologists alike for its dark and tragic portrait of old age. Quite a few years ago it was allowed to go out of print.

Two examples of its hostile reception in the United States are particularly worth noting. In a long, lucid, and reasonable piece that appeared in *The New Yorker*, Robert Coles complained that Beauvoir stresses grim and even horrifying accounts of old age at the expense of arguments and observations that would oppose her conclusions, pointing out that she is deplorably tendentious and one-sided in her choice of the elite class of elderly people—well-known philosophers, statesmen, and writers—from whom she quotes; in rebuttal he offered persuasive and even moving accounts from older Americans from a lower social and economic class who by their own testimony do not despise their old age.[8] Even sharper in his attack than Coles was Robert Butler himself who charged Beauvoir with self-pity and with hatred of the aging person in herself.[9] He criticized her elision of aging with disease and her inability to see aging as a natural process rather than an ontological insult. He faulted her, in other words, for not seeing the human life span as something whole.

I am sympathetic to the criticisms of *The Coming of Age* offered by both Coles and Butler but I think that their violent antipathy to Beauvoir's important book was also in part a response to her dismissal of the role of memory in the elderly in constituting identity. As their own reviews of her book as well as others show, in the atmosphere of the seventies with its valorization of the life review—and its emphasis on the value of creative writing and artplay both for the elderly and by the elderly—Beauvoir's rejection of the meaningful uses of memory was especially scandalous if not altogether taboo.

For Butler, implicitly if not explicitly, conferring dignity on reminiscence in the elderly as individuals and restoring status to the elderly as a group in American society were different aspects of the same project, inextricably linked. For Beauvoir they emphatically were not. Thus a critical consideration of Beauvoir's view of memory may help us not only put her position in perspective but Butler's as well. For in *The Coming of Age* Beauvoir, who to my knowledge never erred on the side of sentimentality or paternalism in her life, asks some of the same questions posed by Butler in his essay on the life review: Why are the elderly so concerned with their pasts? Why do they dwell on memories of their youth? To what degree can the aged recover their pasts? But the tone of her answers is different. I say tone and not substance because her basic insights in this regard are, like Butler's, psychoanalytic as well as social. Both agree that at the root of an elderly person's interest in his past is his evaluation of his life in the present (which implies a question about satisfaction) and the imminence of death. But as a psychiatrist in an Eriksonian tradition, Butler is positive about the role of reminiscence in one's life—and in shaping one's death. As an existentialist and chronicler of the times Beauvoir is not. Both views, it is important to note, are extreme and do not so much serve as correctives to one another as reminders to us that theory is inevitably historically and culturally situated and thus limited in ways that we should take care to understand.

At the same time as Beauvoir's attitude toward remembrance of things past in the elderly will be useful to us as a foil to Butler's notion of the life review, we should also seek to understand the sources of her view (they may be personal as well as cultural) and the contradictions in her work, inquiring if we may find therein any lessons for those of us in the field of gerontology. In what follows I shall be primarily concerned to elucidate Beauvoir's view toward reminiscence in *The Coming of Age*, with reference to her memoirs of her own life as well as her memoirs of the last years of her lifelong companion Jean-Paul Sartre and the last months and days of her mother.

II

For Beauvoir one's identity is created by one's actions. One is defined by what one calls one's "projects" or "activities." Thus in her pioneering book *The Second Sex* which appeared decades before *The Coming of Age*, she argues that a woman can achieve true selfhood only through production, not *re*production. Anything that has to do with a woman's biological self has nothing to do with the authentic creation of her self. As Beauvoir writes in *The Second Sex*, "giving birth and suckling are not *activities*, they are natural *functions*; no project is involved."[10] What is important here for our consideration of the life review is Beauvoir's total rejection of a certain kind of work (here bearing and caring for children) that can be associated with a definite biological age in life (here the span between the onset of puberty and menopause in women). For at the foundation of Butler's theory of the life review is the assumption that old age is indeed a distinct stage in the biological life of a person—one characterized by the sense of the ending of the narrative of one's life—that has to do precisely with the authentic creation of the self. From this perspective we can see the theory of the life review as a specific case of the more general position, if you will, that biology is destiny. Beauvoir, of course, fought against this essentially conservative position all her life—both in terms of feminism and in terms of old age. She has consistently argued that our true selves are not defined by our biological place in life—either in terms of gender or age—but rather by our actions. She does not deny that biology significantly marks our lives. Indeed in terms of advanced old age she stresses to an extreme the physical suffering that it is likely to bring. But she refuses to accord it essentiality or priority. If Butler's theory of the life review is a liberal (if not, in this light, conservative) politics of the psyche, Beauvoir's is a radical politics. There is something heroic in her theoretical gesture of denial. With Dylan Thomas she would have us rage against the dying of the light and not go gentle into that dark night.

Old age is thus for Beauvoir necessarily tragic. In *The Second Sex* she argues that "there is no justification for present existence other than its expansion into an indefinitely open future"; to fall from *transcendence* into *immanence* is "stagnation," "a degradation of existence," "an absolute evil" (xxxiii). Women are urged to create themselves, to transcend their biological place. Similarly in *The Coming of Age* she argues that the elderly must transcend their biological place. But here the similarity ends. With old age Beauvoir encounters the absolute end of the possibility of infinite transcendence or the creation of the self. Her existentialism runs into a dead end: death. The doublebind is this: the elderly can only escape stagnation by projects but those very projects require "an indefinitely open future." Projects are necessarily future-oriented but the future is precisely what the elderly lack. They are doomed. In Beauvoir's terms, the tragedy of old age has an ontological dimension that can never be truly escaped because the very definition of old age is that one is at the end of one's life span and no longer possesses a future.[11]

We should not be surprised to learn that this view of old age as defined by the foreclosure of time and death resonates with Beauvoir's perception of her own experience, or better, her sense of her own truncated future. As we learn from reading her memoirs, even rather early on in her life she came to feel that the future was closed to her. She repeats again and again that the body of her work is essentially formed. To write another book would be merely additive. It would not appreciably change that body of work which is the true gauge of her identity. If in Beauvoir's terms the sense of the present depends on the promise of the future, then the foreclosure of the future means that the past has accumulated in such a measure as to overwhelm the present. Thus she repeatedly describes the past—for herself as well as for the elderly per se—as a weight, a burden that grows heavier as we grow older, as a prison that slowly and inevitably circumscribes the self.

In *The Coming of Age* Beauvoir exhorts the elderly to pursue projects and activities (by this she means primarily work that would contribute to the cultural or political life of the community) but she cannot be sanguine about the outcome. In old age one's biological place is one's biological *fate*. She recounts with genuine admiration the myriad activities of people (Clemenceau, Hugo, Goya, Lou Andreas-Salome, among them) who continued to be astonishingly productive, as we would say, in their old age. But the overall effect is finally not so much inspiring as it is stultifying. What was theoretically a heroic tragedy recedes in the individual case into a stolid pathos.

This is, too, the tone of her memoir of the final ten years in the life of Sartre, the celebrated French philosopher and activist who was her life-long companion and who died at the age of seventy-four after a medical history of several strokes, diabetes, encroaching blindness, and, finally, uremia. In *Adieux: A Farewell to Sartre* Beauvoir insists on his continuing political work (she considers it natural where many of us would find the level of his activity remarkable) and his alternating rhythm of adapting to and resisting his physical limitations, or as he called them, his illnesses (she prefers the mode of aggressivity to that of acceptance or resignation).[12]

Yet despite the fact that Sartre is putatively the hero of her narrative (she dedicates the book: "To those who loved Sartre, who do love him, who will love him"), there is ultimately something relentlessly clinical and colorless about her account. Perhaps it is because she mixes but cannot blend the details of his public life as an influential spokesman for the Left with the banal details of his private life (his anxiety about his dentures, his incontinence, the fact that it took him two days to read the newspaper, his dribbling of his food). Perhaps it is because the narrative is told as a series of "transformations" and "resurrections" against "the irreversible deterioration of age." Beauvoir herself, in other words, could not accept his old age and thus as readers we feel some pity for Sartre and some small smattering of a dislike for her. Perhaps, simply, because Beauvoir is unflinching in her gaze at his aging body and mind when we would be more comfortable with discretion so as to preserve the public Sartre in our memories. Although she writes of her own emotions—her dread, her anguish, her anxiety—she does not in my judgment *evoke* them. Her realism, so to speak, is ultimately dispassionate, unrelieved by the sublimity of the tragic or the companionship of the comic. There can be no hero who is larger than life in this story. Nor will Beauvoir tell this story as a sentimental tale of woman caring for—and taking care of—an old and sick man.

Sartre's experience in his last few years almost uncannily confirmed Beauvoir's views in *The Coming of Age* with respect to activity (the measure of one's identity) and memory. Just as Sartre's values and way of life seem to have served in great part as the basis for her own, so his old age corresponded in perfect detail to the theoretical portrait of old age which we find in *The Coming of Age*. As she tells us in *Adieux*, "Sartre had always lived with his eyes fixed on the future; he could not live otherwise. Now that he was limited to the present, he looked upon himself as dead. Old, threatened in his own body, half-blind, he was shut out from the future" (119-20). One anecdote in particular illustrates this succinctly. Because of his failing health, several years before he died Sartre moved from his tenth-floor walk-up to an apartment with an elevator. Unfortunately this move coincided with his growing blindness which made reading and writing—that is, work, a project—virtually impossible for him. He never felt at home in his last apartment: "*this apartment*," he said, "*is the place where I don't work anymore*"(64). But as I have already mentioned, Sartre's last years were characterized by extreme oscillations in his health and his moods. As Beauvoir records:

> We went back to Paris on September 22, and Sartre returned without pleasure to that dwelling where he "no longer worked." Sylvie went there to spend an evening and he said to her, "Have you come to see the dead man's house?" And a little later, when I questioned him, he replied, "Why, yes, I'm a living corpse." This was before he had returned to any activity. Once he had done so he was much more living than dead. We went on with our dialogues [they were working on a project together] and he said that he was completely *happy*. (73-74)

Significantly, in the one hundred and some pages of her memoir of Sartre Beauvoir never writes of his musing on his past or of his concern with his life as a whole. Reminiscence in Butler's sense was not, it seems, a part of Sartre's experience of old age.

If one of the predominant tropes of the life review is the figure of reconciliation, of the ends of a life being knitted together, in Beauvoir we do not find the satisfactions of resolution. Indeed we encounter the opposite: identity is not solidified, as it were, in the old age of frailty but rather evacuated. Beauvoir, for example, describes Sartre as being himself only when he was well, that is, when he was *like* what he was *before*.[13] Of course we commonly talk about people who are ill this way; the return to health is often described as a return to oneself. But although there may be the strength of courage in refusing to admit illness as part of one's identity, to deny selfhood to the frail, on the other hand, may dispossess them of themselves, of their selves which have now changed. We should note too that here Butler is entirely correct. Beauvoir conceives of the long stretch of old age as a condition of disability which it assuredly need not necessarily be.

For Beauvoir memory is by its very nature the antithesis of the future-oriented project. Although I applaud her refusal to allow our identity to be determined by biology, she errs in her one-dimensional portrayal of memory-work. In her single-minded effort to give the elderly freedom, she reproduces precisely the stereotypical portrait of exasperating old men and women who endlessly repeat the same stories, a stereotype which Butler so brilliantly called into question. Worse, she is contemptuous of the elderly who turn their inner gaze to their pasts. In *The Coming of Age* she writes: old people "set up a fixed unchanging essence against the deteriorations of age, and tirelessly they tell stories of this being that they were, this being that lives on inside them"(538). For Beauvoir reminiscence is an ignoble means of escape: "Once they have recovered him [a former self], once they have merged with him, it does not matter whether they are thirty or fifty or even eighty, they have escaped from old age" (538-39). Here we see just how segmented and discontinuous her view of the human life span is. For Beauvoir the child we once were is "unchanging" and "fixed" and out of weakness we call up that past self against the ignominy of old age and death. The implication is that the self one was as a child is in such a case a *substitute* for what one is now. But at the same time Beauvoir would perpetuate the identity which for her characterizes the long spans of young adulthood and middle age into old age.

Butler in contrast conceives of the psyche as a dynamic system whose elements—our various selves at various points in time—are potentially available and, more importantly, integratable. In Butler's words (the italics are mine), the life review is "a naturally occurring, universal process characterized by the *progressive return* to consciousness of past experiences, and, particularly, the resurgence of *unresolved* conflicts; simultaneously, and normally, these revived experiences and conflicts can be surveyed and *reintegrated*" (66). For Butler reminiscence is a process which in itself is a constructive and creative activity that works to give a final shape to the self. More radically, he posits that the life review is universal and normative. But Beauvoir rejects this, as she rejects all theories of necessary stages that are rooted in biology. Just as she refuses to lend cultural dignity to childbearing for women—her fight for feminism lay elsewhere—so she denies on theoretical grounds that reminiscence can play a critical role in one's "authentic" life when one is old or near death.

If for Beauvoir the necessary if impossible fiction to sustain one's self into and through old age must be a sense of the future, for Butler one's final possession—for him it is no fiction but a truth—is the narrative of one's life, the final version of one's past. In the matter of reminiscence they are theoretically worlds apart. Beauvoir's work serves in this context to remind us that the essentially meditative or psychoanalytic mode honored by Butler is based in biology and founded on a certain model of the mind. And in her *struggle* against the limitations of biology – in this case the deteriorations which almost inevitably accompany advanced old age – she reminds us that in his essay on the life review Butler's mode is essentially that of *acceptance* of one's place in life. Thus their two views represent opposing cultural and personal choices regarding aging in Western society. They also represent different forms of history. If I may borrow a distinction made by the French historian Michel Foucault, following Nietzsche, Butler's notion of the life review is based on:

> the form of history that reintroduces (and always assumes) a suprahistorical perspective: a history whose function is to compose the finally reduced diversity of time into a totality fully enclosed upon itself; a history that always encourages subjective recognitions and attributes a form of reconciliation to all the displacements of the past; a history whose perspective on all that precedes it implies the end of time, a completed development.[14]

To this form of history Beauvoir in *The Coming of Age* stands opposed. Her use of history is dissociative and directed against personal identity as representative of (the dominant) tradition.

III

Throughout her life Beauvoir's overriding concern was social oppression, not psychic repression; liberation and freedom, not happiness. With Sartre she rejected *la vie interieure*, or the inner life. As I have suggested, her view of reminiscence is linked to her existential posture. But she devalues reminiscence, I think, for much more personal reasons as well, reasons that have to do as much with the *texture* of her mind as with the *logic* of her philosophy of life. Such an inquiry into the biases of temperament is in my judgment especially valuable in a field as young and complex as gerontology (we often, for example, seem stuck, unknowingly, in polar binaries such as: old age is good, old age is bad). For it is certain that many people working and writing in the field of aging studies project their hopes and fears—or reproduce aspects of their own temperament—onto that inchoate period to which we affix the label "old age." Important as it is, Beauvoir's own work is a case in point.

In *The Coming of Age* Beauvoir asks: to what *degree* can the elderly recover time past? This is a strange way to pose this question, strange because it implies a scientific, objective, quantitative criterion for measuring the success of an individual's memory. Thus as we see, Beauvoir's notion of memory here is not located in the domain of the psychological—in remembrance or reminiscence in Butler's sense—but rather in the domain of information retrieval.[15] But if reminiscence in the psychological sense holds little interest for her, *social memory* is accorded a high value. What is this kind of memory for Beauvoir? In *The Coming of Age* she describes it as "an intellectual operation that reconstructs and localizes past facts, basing itself on physiological data, images and a certain knowledge, and making use of logical categories. This is the only one that allows us to some degree, to tell ourselves our own history" (539). What kind of history or story would that be? For Beauvoir the act of remembering is not fundamentally a matter of considering—or reconsidering—one's relationship to one's past (to one's mate, work, children, parents, or God) in terms of *affect*. In Beauvoir the psychological work of reminiscence (in Butler's theory the coming to terms with past conflicts) is converted into what is in her view a *project*, a social history. As we see in her four memoirs about her own life—*Memoirs of a Dutiful Daughter, The Prime of Life, Force of Circumstance,* and *All Said and Done*[16]—she takes herself as a document of the times.

How can we be assured that this "history" will be told well, that is, accurately? Of all conditions the most important for Beauvoir—and this shows us just how far we have come from Butler's world—is that the *history must have already been recorded*. This is not a paradox. What Beauvoir means by this is in fact quite literal. The "facts" of the history must already have been set down. This is completely in accord with Beauvoir's practice as a writer. She kept voluminous diaries, and in preparing to write her memoirs (her method is not meditative but bibliographical) she spent days, she tells us, in the Bibliothèque Nationale reading old newspapers and journals, immersing herself in the period of her memoir, refreshing her memory of the public record. As she confesses in a fascinating passage in *The Prime of Life*, her lifelong secret dream was not to possess the complete record of every detail of her life, not to discover the pattern of her past: "*I have always had the secret fantasy that my life was being recorded, down to the tiniest detail, on some tape recorder, and that the day would come when I should play back the whole of my past*" (59). Thus her memoirs deliver a chronicle of the past in a numbing monotone—lists of important cultural figures, itemizations of the plays and movies she saw in any given year, catalogues of recent political events in France, details of her trips abroad.

For Beauvoir memory is a form of archival research, clinical in nature and subject to cross-checking. In *The Coming of Age* she writes—oddly in my judgment—of recovering the past much as would a scientist or logician: "With the help of reasoning, comparison and cross-checking, it is possible to set a certain number of hypotheses that cannot always be verified" (541). The tragedy of memory in old age is not only of psychoanalytic proportions; as one grows older one's memory is necessarily and increasingly subject to error. More precisely, her view of memory is pictorial: the further we stand from a painting, the less likely we are to perceive it with clarity; analogously, the further we are from an event in the past, the less likely we are to discern its details. Unlike Butler, Beauvoir has no theory of perspective, no sense of a time and space needed to see clearly, no belief in wisdom achieved over time. For her, the past is not open to interpretation or rewriting from the stance of the present. A hermeneutics of the past, such as Butler's, is unthinkable. The elderly are thus doubly damned: they lack a future and they lack an unobstructed vision of the past (which at the same time, as we saw earlier, has accumulated around them like so much rubble).

Here we might speculate that her conviction that memory dims over time was related to the very texture of her own mind, which as it is manifested in her writing is immensely literal and logical, as well as to her fears of aging and old age. The fact that Beauvoir was never able to write autobiography, only memoirs, lends support to this view. Out of a sense of anxiety and responsibility she felt compelled to record events and feelings as they occurred because she was certain that later they would be inaccessible. As we read in the Introduction to *Force of Circumstance* (her third volume of memoirs, published when she was fifty-five), she believed that in her old age, whether it was, in her words, "serene or sour," that "the influence of decrepitude would keep me from grasping my subject: the moment when, hard upon a vibrant past, the decline sets in" (xv). Throughout her memoirs what may at first appear to be an interpretive impulse to autobiography turns out to be the wish to paint an accurate portrait of herself at an earlier age. More radically, at times Beauvoir believed that an earlier self had disappeared entirely. If in *The Prime of Life*, for example, she could refer to one of her earliest childhood memories (it had come back to her with force in her thirties), in *Force of Circumstance* (which appeared only two years later) she can no longer grasp the child she once was. Poignantly she tells us, "*The little girl whose future has become my past no longer exists. There are times when I want to believe I still carry her inside me. . . . She has disappeared without leaving even a tiny skeleton to remind me that she once did exist*" (271-72).

As Beauvoir once confessed, "I don't have very warm, lively memories of what happened to me in the past."[17] As her memoirs themselves suggest, her own relationship to her past was not a particularly private or introspective one. They present us with a portrait of a woman for whom coming to terms with her past is not an important concern, with a well-adjusted, confident woman who—at least at the times that she wrote them—does not need to do the work of psychic integration presupposed by the notion of the life review. Like Sartre, Beauvoir would seem to harbor almost no discernable nostalgia for the past. Nor does she lament the past.[18] It was the future—old age and death—that obsessed her.

In Beauvoir's effort to place memory in the public world, she does ignore the rich psychological dimensions of remembrance of things past. In *The Coming of Age* she makes the mistake of projecting the mode her own mind takes onto memory and the elderly in general, concluding that for everyone images of the past are impoverished, colorless, and insipid, and that they become only more so the older we grow. Here we see the danger of attributing to old age per se the attitudes, beliefs, and texture of mind peculiar to oneself.

Yet as we have seen Beauvoir herself appeared to have had no need for—and no personal experience of—the life review. Thus for all its misguided contempt, her view of memory in *The Coming of Age*, when taken together with her memoirs, does remind us that in recent years the life review has been overly generalized and romanticized. Indeed the life review may be a convenient and pleasant fiction embraced by some who wish to give, so to speak, the elderly something meaningful to do. We realize that if Butler's essay were to appear as if for the first time today, it might very well be absorbed as part of our cultural moment with its strange emphasis in both the popular press and gerontological circles on successful aging.

IV

It is of course somewhat ironic that the very person who inveighed against the return to the past that marks the lives of so many elderly people should have written so many volumes of memoirs herself. I have taken pains to point out how different the motive of her memoirs is from the impulse of autobiography and the life review. Yet we must also admit that there are contradictions here. And while there is nothing unusual about finding contradictions between a person's work and her experience, between her theory and her practice, and while we should not fault Beauvoir for these contradictions, we can benefit from understanding them. Two examples, the first of which is particularly important, may be instructive.

Of all Beauvoir's books, *A Very Easy Death*, the memoir of her elderly mother's death from cancer, is the most accomplished in terms of style, structure, voice, and subtlety of observation.[19] It is also the most autobiographical and reflective. In this book Beauvoir does review and remember the past, both her past and her mother's past. The pages of this book are as much about herself as they are about her mother. In them Beauvoir discovers—or should we say, she creates—a meaning to her mother's death and a pattern to her own life. But when she refers, later, to her mother's death in *All Said and Done* she reduces it to a colorless and unambiguous event that serves to illustrate the threats of medical technology. In both *All Said and Done* and *The Coming of Age* she does not *remember* that her pressing need to write about herself and her mother in *A Very Easy Death*—her urgency to establish a close bond between herself and her mother just at the time she was irrevocably slipping away from her—is precisely in the mode of psychic work which she would deny to the elderly.

A Very Easy Death is the literary embodiment of a life review occasioned by the death of one's parent. In spite of Beauvoir's theoretical and temperamental disposition against the life review, one of her very books suggests that for some of us in midlife or older, it may be the death of one's parent which occasions a life review. For it is only in this book that Beauvoir allows the past as it were to have an effect on the present. It is only in *A Very Easy Death* (the title is ambiguous) that she permits a reciprocity between the past and the present. And I must emphasize the fact that there is nothing sentimental about this book. Unlike her plodding and grim memoir of Sartre, in this book Beauvoir is fully present, and she is eloquent.

As for my second example, in *All Said and Done* (published only two years after *The Coming of Age* where she rejected reminiscence) Beauvoir on the contrary admits to the pleasures of reminiscence. Her concern in her early sixties is in "recovering my life—reviving forgotten memories, re-reading, re-seeing, rounding off incomplete pieces of knowledge, filling gaps, clarifying obscurities, gathering scattered elements together. Just as though there had to be a study on the moment when my experience was to be summed up, and as though it mattered that this summing-up should be done" (48). She writes warmly of her long life in Paris—it is a place abundant in memories for her—and she tells us that she has always taken great pleasure in talking over old times with her sister, with Sartre, and with her friends. If before she vehemently denied any link between memory and reminiscence, now she embraces it and her concern with the past and in particular with the final shaping—"the summing-up"—of the narrative of her life sounds very similar indeed to Butler's notion of the life review. As we read, "the nearer I come toward the end of my days, the more I am enabled to see that strange thing a life, and to see it whole" (7). Yet Beauvoir does not seem to be aware that this represents a fundamental change in her thinking. In this matter her thought lacks dialectical insight. And soon after the first few chapters, incipient autobiography breaks down into the half-life and soon thereafter into the quarter-life of the march of events. What seemed to have begun as a life review in Butler's terms devolves into a chronicle, a recitation of events, a diary.

Beauvoir's inability to see this contradiction—to take into account the lie her experience gave to her theory over time—is, I think, related to her view of the human life course as ideally unchanging. As I have already mentioned, Beauvoir factored out biology as a critical dimension in the creating of a person's identity. She never considered seriously theories of psychological stages in human development such as those proposed by Erik Erikson. She never seems to have been impressed by the basic truth that we do—and we desire to do—different things at different points in our lives. It is telling that as a child one fairy tale in particular enchanted her: the story of Charlotte, who shrinks to miniature proportions and then swells to gigantic dimensions. As a little girl Beauvoir imagined herself to be Charlotte and commented in *Memoirs of a Dutiful Daughter* with palpable relief: "I came out of the adventure safe and sound after having been reduced to a foetus and then blown up to matronly dimensions" (8). Almost obsessively she associates the miniature and the gigantesque with changes in the body, with a condition to be feared and avoided, with, in short, pregnancy and motherhood. Surely it cannot be insignificant that neither as an adolescent nor as an adult did she ever see motherhood as part of her future.

The work of Beauvoir reminds us that one of the hazards of the field of aging studies is that we may project onto old age our own fantasies, fears, and life experience of our early and middle years. If as a woman in late middle age committed to the tenets of existentialism the author of *The Coming of Age* counselled the elderly to remain involved in the projects of their middle years, we should also note that here too she was projecting onto old age the way she had led her own life up to age sixty. Despite Beauvoir's transformation early on from a solitary university student into a celebrated public figure, her life is remarkable for its *lack* of change. As she was fond of observing, she lived her entire life in the same "village" on the Left Bank of Paris. Since her twenties Sartre was, until his death, her constant companion. Throughout her adult years she pursued the same occupation—writing and political activity on the Left—and has had many life-long friendships. Perhaps most importantly, her life was never punctuated by the birth and growth of children. It was, in other words, been distinguished by immense continuity—no violent ruptures, no real dislocations. Thus Beauvoir's own experience reinforced her philosophical conviction that the ideal life span is unmarred by intrusive change, whether by this we mean biological change (puberty, motherhood, old age) or an abandonment of the goals—the projects—defined for oneself as an adult.

V

I have suggested that Butler's brilliant and effective notion of the life review lent itself to sentimentalization which is seen all the more clearly when we compare his view of reminiscence with Beauvoir's view of personal memory. Similarly, in its debased if not degenerate form, Beauvoir's devaluation of personal memory and biological change represents a violent rejection of aging itself which we see exemplified in its technological extreme. It is by no means insignificant that in a country whose population has a larger percentage of elderly people than the United States, a recent issue of the most popular weekly magazine, *Paris Match*, should feature a twelve-page article, complete with doublespread color photographs, on cosmetic surgery to produce "eternal youth." One of the most compelling vignettes is of an older couple who underwent cosmetic surgery together. Faces swollen and bandaged, they are shown in their nightclothes in their hospital room holding hands and smiling not at each other but at the camera. As the text comments, "If 'growing old together' is the promise upon which marriage is founded, today 'growing younger together' is a realistic basis for those who wish to prolong the happiness of being attractive to each other and of giving each other pleasure."[20] The aging body is to be—on the surface at least—literally effaced, left behind in the past, forgotten.

But cultural moments are complex. The existentialist moment in France is long past. As a gesture toward conclusion I refer the reader to *Childhood*, the marvellous autobiography of Nathalie Sarraute's early years which was published in France in 1983 when she was eighty-three.[21] Mindful, indeed painfully self-conscious of the dangers of sentimentality, the book opens with a dialogue between two voices—one warning that the desire to return to one's past in reminiscence, the wish to evoke one's memories in writing, is an embarrassment and worse, a possible sign of declining forces (it could almost be Beauvoir speaking); the other voice pulled by the past, toward her first memory, a vivid scene of defiance and violence, of Sarraute as a little girl disobeying her strict German tutor, of a child deliberately slashing a pillow with scissors. The first voice checks the second: isn't it too sentimental? But the second voice, the now-confident voice, continues with her memories—especially with memories of her mother who abandoned her in Paris and returned to Russia—which are stunning in their theatricality and insight. Sarraute remembers, for example, the moment when she first sensed that something—it was a doll—was more beautiful than her mother. About her relationship to her mother, she comes to understanding if not acceptance: "How long did it take you to realize that she never tried—unless very absentmindedly and clumsily—to put herself in your place?" (19). Unlike Beauvoir, Sarraute knows that what you evoke, finally, are not facts or even scenes but your feelings—of fear, of fascination, of joy, repulsion, embarrassment. Unerringly she escapes the sentimental, understanding with the British psychoanalyst D.W. Winnicott that sentimentality is a quality that arises from the repression of hatred, from the inability to acknowledge that one is capable of hatred. Sarraute's moving book, like Beauvoir's *A Very Easy Death*, is a consummate embodiment of what the late French writer Roland Barthes has called *anamnesis*, "the action—a mixture of pleasure and effort—performed by the subject in order to recover, *without magnifying or sentimentalizing it*, a tenuity of memory,"[22] here a review of one's life.

NOTES

1. Robert Coles, *The Old Ones of New Mexico* (Garden City: New York: Anchor Books, 1975).
2. Robert Butler, "The Life Review: An Interpretation of Reminiscence in the Aged," *Psychiatry* 26.1 (February 1963): 65-76.
3. Kathleen Woodward, "Reminiscence and the Life Review: Prospects and Retrospects," *What Does It Mean to Grow Old?: Reflections from the Humanities,* ed. Sally Gadow and Thomas R. Cole (Durham UP, 1986) 137-61.

4. John Vidal, "Theatrical Revival," *Manchester Guardian*, December 17, 1986.

5. Barbara Myerhoff, *Number Our Days* (New York: Dutton, 1978); Kenneth Koch, *I Never Told Anybody: Teaching Poetry Writing in a Nursing Home* (New York: Random House, 1977).

6. Robert Butler, *Why Survive? Being Old in America* (San Francisco: Harper and Row, 1975).

7. Simone de Beauvoir, *The Coming of Age*, trans. Patrick O'Brian (1970; New York: Warner Paperback, 1972).

8. Robert Coles, *The New Yorker*, August 19, 1972, 68ff.

9. Robert Butler, *The Washington Star*, May 28, 1972, G-6, G-7.

10. Simone de Beauvoir, *The Second Sex*, trans. H.M. Parshley (1949; New York: Vintage, 1974) 165.

11. Actually this is changing. Old age is a biological fact and a social construction. Just how these two determinants intertwine at any one historical point is fascinating. With a larger proportion of our population sixty-five and older and with a larger proportion of the elderly population living longer and healthier lives we are coming to realize that old age can be a long span of time indeed. Thus, as in Bernice Neugarten's formulation of the old-old (a category that oscillates between the biological—the frail elderly—and the social—those seventy-five and over), we are in the process in the United States of changing the definition of old age. On the one hand we are pushing it chronologically to a higher figure on the assumption that a long and healthy old age is quite normal; at the same time (here is the contradiction) we are associating old age (the old-old) with decrepitude and frailty. For a valuable contribution to the redefinition of old age see Alan Pifer's "The Public Policy Response," *Our Aging Society*, eds. Alan Piefer and Lydia Bronte (New York: W.W. Norton & Co., 1986):402-5.

12. Simone de Beauvoir, *Adieux: A Farewell to Sartre,* trans. Patrick O'Brian (1981; Harmondsworth, England: Penguin, 1984) 34.

13. As we read early on in *Adieux*, in a parenthesis: "What was so extraordinary about Sartre and so disconcerting for those around him was that he could emerge, cheerful and intact, from the bottom of abysses that seemed to have swallowed him forever. I had wept over him for a whole summer, and yet he had returned entirely to his former state, wholly himself again, as though 'the wing of weakness' had never brushed him." (35). Or as we read later, when Beauvoir is writing about Sartre meeting in 1977 with other political figures about an incident in Italy (a student had been killed in Bologna and there were huge demonstrations): "Sartre had indeed spoken very well. And in our own conversations too, I found him his old self entirely. We talked about our life, about our age, about everything and nothing. He had grown older, certainly, but he was truly himself" (107).

14. Michel Foucault, "Nietzsche, Geneology, History," *Language, Counter-Memory, Practice: Essays and Interviews*, ed. Donald F. Bouchard, trans. Sherry Simon (Ithaca: Cornell UP, 1980) 152.

15. This distinction corresponds to the distinction between *informative* and

evaluative reminiscence made by Marianne Lo Gerfo in "Three Ways of Reminiscence in Theory and Practice," *International Journal of Aging and Human Development* 12.1 (1980-81): 39-48. Interestingly enough, Gerfo's essay itself reveals the extent to which Butler's notion of the life review has been gutted of its bite and sentimentalized: she associates *evaluative* reminiscence with Butler's notion of the life review but emphasizes only the positive outcome—the attainment of ego integrity and the achievement of meaning—and introduces the new category of *obsessive* reminiscence, which for Butler could very well characterize the life review. As she writes, "obsessive reminiscing about a particular situation may not yield life review therapy" (44).

16. Simone de Beauvoir, *Memoirs of a Dutiful Daughter*, trans. James Kirkup (1958; New York: Harper Colophon Books, 1974); *The Prime Life*, trans. Peter Green (1960; New York: Harper and Row, 1976); *Force of Circumstance*, trans. Richard Howard (1962; New York: G.P. Putnam's Sons, 1964); *All Said and Done*, trans. Patrick O'Brian (1972; New York: Warner Books, 1975).

17. Josée Dayan and Malka Ribowska, *Simone de Beauvoir: A Film* (Paris: Gallimard, 1978) 92.

18. Indeed this is one of the very reasons why her memoirs fail as autobiography. They do not seem sufficiently motivated by a need to understand her personal life and are too much connected with the public realm.

19. Simone de Beauvoir, *A Very Easy Death*, trans. Patrick O'Brian (1964; New York: 1966).

20. Jean-Claude Sauer and Roger Picherie, "L'Eternelle jeunesse: les derniers miracles de la chirugie esthétique," *Paris Match*, January 23, 1987, 82-93.

21. Nathalie Sarraute, *Childhood*, trans. Barbara Wright (1983; New York: George Braziller, 1984).

22. Roland Barthes, *RB by RB*, trans. Richard Howard (New York: Hill and Wang, 1977) 109.

Rediscovered Lives: Work with Older People in the Search for Time Past

Peter Sprinkart

In the past two decades or so educational opportunities for seniors have increased in number, variety, and importance to the lives of the participants. Increasingly, gerontological institutions like nursing homes and senior centers have become involved in educational programming—a new field of endeavor for many. In a parallel fashion, growing numbers of traditional colleges and universities now offer programs designed specifically for retirees. There are, of course, many reasons for this educational boom among the elderly, including the recent recognition of old age as a third phase of life; a fundamental change in the goals concerning social work with older adults from that of care and control to one of activitating social integration; and finally a change in the life plans and expectations within a new generation of seniors and social workers alike. From this background, then, educational work with seniors has become an innovative field in which an abundance of interesting models have been tried out.

In the course of these explorations, one of the main problems that comes up for discussion is the question of the kinds of educational opportunity that are most appropriate for seniors in general and especially for those who have had little exposure to formal education.

Peter Sprinkart is Professor of Psychology in the School of Social Work at the University of Munich where he directs a Life Review Project. His publications include *Cognitive Aesthetics*, among numerous books and articles on aging.

This paper was translated by Catherine Hezser and K. Murr.

It seems clear enough—and experience confirms this everywhere—that the traditional educational offerings such as language courses or literature circles are inappropriate for the latter group. It thus becomes necessary to inquire if the classical school-oriented way of learning shouldn't be replaced by new forms of learning based on personal experience. From these considerations, a new type of educational work has gained increasing importance in recent years. In this context, life-history discussion groups represent a newly discovered method. It is obvious that such a narrative approach combines personal development and learning by experience in an extraordinary way. This practice, however, requires a carefully differentiated understanding of group process.

The present essay tries to bring about such an understanding by presenting narrative life history in its everyday social meaning. To describe processes of change evoked by narrative life history, models for the understanding of such processes are taken from psychotherapy. With this as background, in the last part of the essay another form of life-historical methodology taken from social history is analyzed in its possibilities for action and potential for change. The essay begins—how could it be otherwise with such a theme—with a story.

IMPRESSIONS FROM THE OTTAKRINGER GROUP

A hot humid afternoon, the sky is black, a storm is coming. Every Wednesday for the past 3 years a life-history discussion group has met at the Ottakringer Adult Education Center. Today's theme: death and dying. The 15-20 participants are all of an age that knows the strong grip of death on life. Death has already become a part of their lives. Mrs. M's husband, himself a member of the group, died 2 weeks ago. Will his wife join the group on this issue today? She does. Dressed in black, erect. The greeting with the young group leaders—students specializing in social history—takes place affectionately, indicating mutual confidence.

The group begins. A man, Mr. O, reads his own text about partnership which actually has nothing to do with the topic in question. Or does it? Mrs. M is uneasy, Mrs. S puts her arm around Mrs. M and gently strokes her back. Inconspicuously, as a matter of course, without dramatics. Restrained applause as Mr. O finishes reading his text.

The leaders guide the group back to the topic by reading aloud a letter from a member who couldn't attend today's session and yet with the letter wishes to contribute to the session. It begins: "My dear friends" and ends: "Man is born, man must die." Bewildered silences, furtive glances at Mrs. M. She remains calm. Mrs. S holds Mrs. M's hand.

What follows is a well-coordinated ritual that might appear to outsiders as a bizarre "hit parade" of reminiscences about the last hours of life. Transcribed contributions from the previous meeting are rated by each group member, whose decisions are supported by a wide range of argument. Some express sympathy and admiration for the courageous bearing of the hero; others praise the exactness of descriptive detail; another group is enthusiastic about the descriptions of exotic death customs.

The leaders announce that "Mrs. N's contribution receives first prize, second prize goes to Mr. O for his wonderful story about death in the countryside and third place is awarded to Mrs. K because the group liked all her stories." These painstakingly expressed judgments create a paradox between what has been said and the life-reality of the speakers, a density of the absurd reminiscent of Beckett's *Endgame*.

The group proceeds with the day's agenda. After four contributions, Mrs. M becomes nervous; hardly perceptible gestures anticipate her speech. The gestures suffice to silence the other conversations in the room: a sea of frozen words, in which all attention focuses on her. With a clear, even voice, she tells of the months of sickness, of the last days in the hospital, of the last hours of her husband's life. An eyewitness to death. In support of what was said, she insists on passing a photo around showing her and her husband: each person in the circle should see how well he was recovering in those last months, how suddenly death had overtaken him. Often her voice breaks for a moment. Yes, he suspected it, he knew that he would die. Morphine. The son, the grandchildren, the doctors were there. She had known about it for a long time and yet, in spite of everything, those last nine months were happy.

The astounding has occurred. She has spoken. Not just that Mrs.

M came but that she came obviously with the intention of telling the story of her husband's suffering. She broke the spell of well-meaning friendly respect. She had the courage to confront the paralyzing taboo which forces one to keep silent. She dared express the unmentionable.

With regained ease, the group members could then express their words of consolation, now more genuine than the customary ritual phrases. They are stories, they comfort. Sorrows shared become bearable. For example, when Mrs. U tells how, during the post-war years in Vienna, her husband drowned in a water-filled bomb crater just when people were beginning to believe the worst was over. Or when Mr. F speaks about the peaceful dead who, when he held watch one night somewhere on the Russian front, shattered his fear of death.

What began as a strained ritual all of a sudden becomes living psychotherapeutic work: intuitive, precise, and showing feelings of camaraderie.

A different reality enters when one of the leaders, a Chilean, begins to tell how in her homeland people don't believe that the dead exist separately from the living. People there—and the manner in which she says this shows that it is more than just primitive superstition—believe that the dead live with us. People prepare places for them and keep their chairs ready, for they are with us. Everyone looks up; next to Mrs. M, placed slightly towards the back, is an empty chair. Mrs. S holds Mrs. M's hand. "People remain with us as long as we remember them," intones Mr. O, and the tension disappears. Humorous stories on the topic of death are trotted out—schoolboy pranks by an open grave of a farmer or a story about bedbugs populating the apartment whenever someone has died or the story of Mr. Z, who, according to his doctor's opinion, should have died 43 years ago and yet still lives, a proud 81-year-old.

As the meeting comes to an end, Mrs. N is declared winner of this competition. Her name is written as the first on the blackboard; in places 2 and 3, Mr. F and Mrs. O follow. According to the unwritten rules of the group, Mrs. N takes the floor and relates in a brisk yet anxious tone of voice about a health problem: a doctor has ascertained that she has cysts, and that the cysts are spreading. Life is precious and lasts till the day it ends. Carpe diem.

They plan a group walking tour. Mr. K will plan everything and present his plans to the group for their decision. Each member says good-bye. The storm has ended; it is cooler, with a pleasant breeze smelling of spring dampness and fresh green.

There are afternoons similar to this everywhere. In Vienna, Munich, London, in the South Bronx, in Los Angeles, wherever discussion groups of everyday life history have found a place in the work with older adults. What happens during these afternoons? What is the secret behind these seemingly everyday events? What is it that turns afternoons like this into educational events, into places of lively learning? What is it that changes worry-laden, one-dimensional thinking into a mode of thought encompassing more freedom, into a mode of thought which doesn't allow itself through powerlessness to be made speechless, even in the face of death, a mode of thought which in spite of the inevitability of death, generates hope, a joy of living and a healthy perspective on life?

MADELAINES AND LIME FLOWER TEA

A first step on the way toward answering the aforementioned question leads to the insight that narrated life-history, besides its educational usage, is first of all a natural part of everyday life. Madelaines and lime flower tea, as in Marcel Proust's *Remembrance of Things Past*, however, are not absolutely indispensable.

> And just as the Japanese amuse themselves by filling a porcelain bowl with water and steeping in it little crumbs of paper which until then are without character or form, but the moment they become wet, stretch themselves and bend, take on colour and distinctive shape, become flowers or houses or people, permanent and recognizable, so in that moment all the flowers in our garden and in M. Swann's park, and the water-lilies on the Vivonne and the good folk of the village and their little dwellings and the parish church and the whole of Combray and of its surrounding taking their proper shapes and

> growing solid, sprang into being, town and gardens alike, from my cup of tea.[1]

Think about the following examples:

In a class meeting, sedate men and women are carrying on a form of exorcism: the ghosts of long-dead teachers stand embodied in front of the group, the air reeks with floorwax just as it did in school, and the voice of the teacher screams, "Sit—you have failed!" and in this moment each participant imagines himself to have a stomach ache—just as in earlier times.

Seniors who are strangers to each other are sitting on a park bench. They talk about the weather and not long after something unusual happens. Photos are taken out and they begin to narrate. What is being told? Life histories!

Two lovers, with shining eyes, are sitting opposite each other in a restaurant—they have much to tell each other. What are they talking about? Life histories. Each story has not been told before, is new, exciting. Each story opens horizons, lets the other drew near, makes the other dearer.

These examples illustrate how widely spread is this pattern of communication, of telling life histories in everyday life. In trying to understand everyday human behavior some theoreticians go so far as to maintain that in just this type of exchange we gain our personal identities. Educational work, entering into such a meaningful everyday communications pattern, is sustained through a hardly-to-be overestimated motivational power: this pattern is immensely attractive. Biographical work is consequently not confronted with the problem besetting other methods, to motivate the at-first-unwilling participant. It suffices to permit an everyday communications pattern to unfold its own specific dynamic, a dynamic in which a person always tells more than he or she initially wanted to. From each story already begun the next directly follows, as if these stories were pearls hanging on an invisible thread and creating a necklace. In a research project which I am directing at the school of social work at the University of Munich entitled "History and Life History," a girl with a predilection for punk attire is employed. This girl carried out her interviews at a home for the aged wearing a pink and green Mohawk haircut, leather clothes and chains. An interesting phenomenon occurs. She gets interviewees to tell about youthful rebellions in their own lives. A very different life story, perhaps one never told before, emerges because of the special circumstances influencing the interviewer.

To more closely grasp the specific meaning of this communication pattern, that is to describe its particular dynamics more precisely, it is helpful to search for a typology in everyday communicational situations in which certain aspects of life histories are told. As explained above, the telling of stories constitutes a definite form of self-presentation: a spoken life history is, then, always a construction of the past brought to the present. This construction is based on a store of possible stories chosen according to specific criteria at the moment of the telling. Four types of stories can be distinguished:

—First of all, every one of us tells a few, standard biographical stories over and over again. They have become stereotypes like the photos in an album; these stories are carefully chosen and preserved, the whole bound in mental pigskin leather. These are the stories related in social circles again and again as anecdotes, boring one's wife and children.

—Besides these stereotypical stories there are others, which one only tells when specifically asked. These are frequently stories about connections forgotten or not mentioned because of their seeming unimportance. Nevertheless, these situational, question-answering stories are more interesting to the listener than the presumably more important standard stories.

—Next to these two types of stories is the "stock of stories" appropriate only for private hearing. This type of story is annoying, awkward, unfortunate; they cannot be told in everyday situations; the person himself knows that they exist, lives in constant fear of their discovery, and tries even at the cost of lying to prevent their discovery. It goes so far that even people who know that their listeners are acquainted with their private stories tell each other how normal their lives have been. Stories of this type are about illegitimate births, abortions, the Third Reich, etc.

—There is yet another type of story: those that are unknown to oneself as long as the repetitive pattern remained unrecognized. These stories come up when an intelligent listener recognizes such general patterns and thereby forces the storyteller to analyze himself. This can also happen in a group setting where other already told stories question one's own "normal" biography and reveal repressed, forgotten stories.

Oral life history as a method of adult education is above all confronted with an overlay of different types of stories. The deciding question is: which stories initiate personal learning and development and which kind of storytelling offers the best opportunity for change. To answer these two questions, the following begins with a discussion about models of change and their development within psychotherapy.

THE RETURN OF THE SUPPRESSED/REPRESSED

Since Freud, psychotherapy has developed as work on biography realizing that mental illnesses are not illnesses in a medical sense but rather misled formative processes. Since its beginnings, psychotherapy has tried to make these misled formative processes conscious in order to liberate a person from the spell of his own past which limits his present experience and behavior, thereby enabling a future of free choice. This method of concentrating on the realization of conflicts within life history has been practiced not only by classical psychoanalysis but is one of the main, basic axioms shared by all psychotherapeutic schools.

How can the psychotherapeutic dissolution of misled formative processes concentrating upon the narration of life history be determined more precisely? The telling of life histories realizes past experiences. This realization can happen in various ways: by simply designating an experience or by actually reexperiencing it. Someone working with life history recognizes at once when his narration becomes authentic for the storyteller; such people are no longer present in the real world—their eyes go out of focus and the interlocutor does not seem to exist anymore. This striking change in visible behavior might best be designated as a trance-like state. In this connection, it is interesting to note that psychotherapeutic work, at the time when Freud and Breuer wrote their studies on hysteria, began with inducing a hypnotic trance to uncover forgotten experiences which caused mental diseases. During the course of their work, Freud and Breuer discovered that a formal induction to the trance state often is not necessary because the patients—carried away by their stories and the emotions they trigger—fall into a state of auto-suggestion. Freud himself emphasized specifically in his later writings that psychotherapeutic work adheres exclusively to the method of free association and so has nothing in common with the hypnotherapeutic beginnings of psychoanalysis. Nevertheless, even in the analytical process, reconstructions of life history succeed only where the story becomes a realization of past experiences. The goal of analytical work is, indeed, not the reconstruction of life historical events but the actual re-experience of past events in the analytical situation.[2]

This re-experience combines facts with emotions, the rationally reconstructible with irrational aspects creating a closed unit of experience marked by the immediacy of experiences and intermodal remembrances. At the same time, successful remembrances imply that a specific form of transference takes place, that the present, past and future blend into unified narrative timelessness, to a mode in which time no longer plays a constructive or ordering role. Closely linked with this is the observation that where the story is successful, the separation between the narrative "I" or ego of the story and the storyteller, conscious about his narrating, disappears. The story becomes "real." It incarnates the narrated in present reality, manifests the contents of the story—and this is especially emphasized in Freud's psychoanalytic method—in the specific structure of the relation between the storyteller and his listener through reciprocal transference.

By now it should be obvious that successful storytelling is accompanied by a clear transformation of what we call every day consciousness into a trance-like state—a narrowing of consciousness, time regression, diffusion of the limits of the ego, etc. The listener generally notices little of this transformation because he finds himself, when the story is told correctly, also in a trance.[3]

In order to succeed with rendering powerless the restraints operating in a particular life story, especially in stories of the second type, a further step is needed: integration of the heretofore suppressed stories and symbols into the conscious experience of the narration. In the beginnings of psychoanalysis, it was assumed that only the rediscovery and subsequent verbalization of traumatizing experiences could bring about a cleansing of the spirit and a healing of symptoms. In accordance with Aristotle's *Poetics*, this phenomenon was designed as a catharsis. Later it became evident that, in order to prevent a recurrence of symptoms in an altered form, an analysis and clarification of the transference relation is necessary. According to the logic of this explanation, the patterns of relationship noticed by the listener and—with special hints—noticeable also for the narrator can be understood as unconscious repetitions of early childhood patterns of relationship which cause the development of symptoms. Clarification, then, leads to a new meaning. A pattern, which through its repression into the unconscious, returns constantly to bedevil the patient, loses its almost unstoppable power when a change of meaning takes place; thereby, split-off contents, exiled symbols and indicated stories are turned into acceptable experiences. The compulsion toward constant repetition is broken. The basis for this is a change of meaning altering the framework of the experience. In the core of this new interpretation stands a demystification of the individual story. Individual life experiences are integrated through this interpretation into a model of universal narrative structure.

Each historical account, each "special" story, can claim to be unique. A universal interpretation, however, although it never leaves the level of narrative description, breaks the spell of the purely historical. It has the form of a story because it should help individuals to reconstruct their unique life histories in narrative form; but it can only serve as a backdrop for many such stories because it does not apply only to one individual case. It is a systematically generalized story supplying the pattern for many stories with foreseeable alternative outcomes, even though each of these stories can claim to have individual biographical significance.

The basis of this generalization lies in the universal elements of individually told stories.

In every story, be it over so incidental, lies a universal theme. In every story another person can find something exemplary. Stories are understood as exemplary the more typical material they contain. The idea of a "type" indicates a quality of being easily understood: a story is typical in a given situation or with regard to a specific public when the action can easily be taken from its context and transferred to other individualized life situations. The universal interpretation includes no names of individuals, only anonymous roles; it includes no contingent conditions, only recurring configurations and patterns of actions; it includes no idiomatic use of speech, only standardized vocabulary.

The basis for the reinterpretation forms, therefore, a universal life history, which in the case of Freud is centered around the myth of Oedipus as the embodiment of all possible individual stories. It describes no typical event/process but rather in idealized form, the pattern for a single action with hypothetical variations. In this way Freud presented the Oedipus conflict and its solutions with such structural terms as the ego, superego and the id (taken from experiences drawn from analytical discussions); with roles, persons and patterns of interaction (resulting from the family structure); and finally with mechanisms of action and communication (as object choice, identification and internalization).

At this point Jürgen Habermas refers to an interesting sideline, which would be worth following up:

> The terminological use of ordinary language is not just an attribute of an accidental stage in the development of psychoanalysis. Rather all attempts to provide metapsychology with a more rigorous form have failed, because the conditions of the application of general interpretations exclude the formalization of ordinary language which the analyst and the patient make use of in completing an analytic narrative scheme by making it into a history. By putting individual names in the place of anonymous roles and filling out interaction patterns as experienced scenes, they develop ad hoc a new language, in which the language of general interpretation is brought into accord with the patient's own language.
>
> The interpretation of a case is corroborated only by the successful continuation of a self-formative process, that is by the completion of self-reflection, and not in any unmistakable way by what the patient says or how he behaves. Here success and failure cannot be intersubjectively established, as is possible in the framework of instrumental action or that of communicative

> action, each in its way. Even the disappearance of symptoms does not allow a compelling conclusion. For they may have been replaced by other symptoms that at first are inaccessible to observation or the experience of interaction. For the symptom, too, is bound in principle to the meaning that it has for the subject engaged in defense. It is incorporated in the structure of self-objectivation and self-reflection and has no falsifying or verifying power independent of it. Freud is conscious of this methodological difficulty. He knows that the "no" of the analysand and rejecting a suggested construction is ambiguous.
>
> Freud is thinking of the confirming associations of the dreamer, who brings up previously forgotten text fragments or produces new dreams. On the other hand, doubt then arises whether the dreams have not been influenced by suggestion on the part of the physician.
>
> Freud is convinced that the physician's suggestion finds its limit in the mechanism of dream formation, which cannot be influenced. Still, the analytic situation attributes a special significance not only to the patient's "No" but to his "Yes" as well. For even the patient's confirmations cannot be taken at face value. Some critics charge that the analyst merely induces a modification of a previous interpretation of life history by talking the patient into a new terminology.
>
> Even indirect confirmation by association only has a relative value when considered in isolation. Freud is right in insisting that only the further course of analysis can decide a construction's usefulness or lack of it. Only the context of the self-formative process as a whole has confirming and falsifying power.[4]

Since Freud, it has become clear that the limitation of the reconstruction of life history to only one story is too narrow. The history of the psychoanalytic movement itself shows its dissatisfaction with this limitation. Adler's criticism or Jung's introduction of a multitude of collective myths show possibilities of an extension of the narrative models of interpretation. Undisputed in all these approaches is, however, the emphasis on reinterpretation for the process of therapeutic change.

There are two important characteristics of change-oriented work with life history within psychotherapy:

- on the one hand, the observation that the realization of the story is a precondition for change;
- on the other hand, the necessity of a universal life history as a basis for a new interpretation, that is, a demystification of individual biographical experience.

Only where these two aspects intersect can an individual formative process emerge as emancipatory self-reflection. And only then can the tyranny of the past be rendered powerless.

SOCIAL-HISTORICAL QUESTIONS AS A METHOD OF BIOGRAPHICAL WORK

With the preceding as background, I want to analyze a biographical model which takes social history as its point of departure. Basically, this model uses Wappelshammer and Weber's text on social history, a work which shows the crucial significance of such common turning points in life as birth, childhood, school, choice of occupation, the beginning of work, love and partner selection, leaving the parental home, marriage, the setting up of a separate household, life crises, social contacts, old age and the balance of life.[5] This choice of the starting point—the social-historical work with life histories—is utilized by other biographically-oriented methods. Characteristic of this form of work is the use of a standardized set of questions around a pre-determined theme.

Each subject area can be divided into further areas for questioning. The prepared list of questions does not have to be slavishly adhered to; rather, it helps in the beginning to keep the group's conversation from straying from the topic. We recommend the following questions as a rough outline for all topics:

- Describe what life was like in the "old days" (for yourself and others).
- How would you evaluate life in those days?
- Describe what life is like today (for yourself and others).
- How would you evaluate life today?

The central principle behind this method of questioning is not so much the attempt to reconstruct actual conditions, but rather to elicit comparisons between today and yesterday, between the narrator and the other, between events and their meaning. It has been stated above that reinterpretation is an essential, methodical step in change-oriented psychotherapeutic work; likewise, for the analysis of the social historical approach to history, it can be assumed that this form of comparative questioning creates a basis for a reinterpretation of life-historical experience. In the way it is commonly related, life historical experience does not clearly differentiate between the present and the past, between the storyteller and the others, between actual experiences and their meaning; the reworking of life history experiences, with the help of a questionnaire which clearly differentiates between past and present, the storyteller and his social world, facts and social norms can create the basis for a reinterpretation of experience. The aspect of comparison between today and yesterday reveals how events of the past overlay the present just as it shows the possibility of emerging from the constraints of the past. The exactness with which this method of questioning separates past from present has the effect of ending the compulsion towards constant repetition of past events. The aspect of comparison between the storyteller and the other reveals how social factors condition an individual's life story. At the same time, it enables the storyteller to see his uniqueness, his individuality: life history is liberated from the stains of personal wrongdoings without turning them into an ominous power of fate. The process of comparing actual events and their meaning liberates the storyteller from the entanglements in which they are held by the potency of colloquial language.

Further, the fixed reality of individual biographical experience disclosed by the method of social-history questions gains importance when accompanied by knowledge of the social-historical background from which the storyteller emerged and grew. This knowledge permits the integration of individual biographical experience into a generalized narrative of past events. In this sense, the social-historical approach functions in a way similar to the logic of psychoanalysis: it furthers the objectification of biographical experience already initiated by this kind of questioning. At the same time, this knowledge offers insight into another essential dimension: personal identity in relation to the social group. At this point social-historical work with life history becomes a form of learning in which personal formative processes and political awarenesses coincide. The objectified reinterpretation of individual biographical experience can then form the basis of a social as well as a personal identity.

SUMMARY AND CONCLUSIONS

According to the theoretical considerations discussed above and to much clinical experience, the genuine actualization of past experiences in the narrative process is a necessary pre-condition for successful life review. In fact, it is only where the past becomes alive for the storyteller that it is possible for beneficial change to occur. Within the framework of the social-historical approach to life history, the group leader's effectiveness in helping the storyteller to provide a detailed account of the actual conditions and arrangements of everyday life is essential if the client is to reach a mental state in which the past is fully realized. If the storyteller follows the pathway established by the leader, he will eventually reach a state in which the narrated situation is enriched by those deeper spheres which are censured by the conscious ego. (Without this assistance it is difficult, if not impossible, for the storyteller to make these advances.) If at this moment the storyteller can experience the essence of his/her story, domination by ancient habits of thought can be challenged and the teller freed to fully experience the present. He who has learned to understand the meaning of his own silence has already started talking.

Narrated history as a method of work with older adults enables—as has already been said—individual processes of change to occur.

It also brings to life a multitude of already forgotten stories. Why? In order to pass them on to future generations!

If educational work using individual life history does not want to become the victim of a hypocritical ideology of privacy, these stories must be integrated into the collective memory that we usually call history. History from down under, then, has two meanings: first, the well-known notion of L. Niethammer's that "a democratic future needs a past in which not only the upper class is heard from." History from down under, however, means also that history does not confine life-historical experience to the limits of consciousness. History from down under, in this second sense, denotes a history derived from the deeper levels of our consciousness, a history not ashamed to listen to and to pass on those stories which go beyond the pale of what social scientific open-mindedness and respectability consider possible and desirable.

NOTES

1. Marcel Proust, *Swann's Way*, trans. by C. Scott Moncreiff, New York: Modern Library, 1956, p. 66.

2. "In the earliest days of the development of analytical technique from an intellectual point of view we highly valued the patient's knowledge of what he had forgotten and thereby scarcely differentiated between our knowledge and the patient's own. We considered it a stroke of good luck when we succeeded in obtaining information about forgotten childhood traumas from another point of view, for example, from parents, caretakers or from the seducer himself . . . and hurried to bring to the patient's attention the news and the evidence of its accuracy in the certain expectation to bring to a quick end the neurosis and its treatment. It was a great disappointment when the expected success didn't occur. How could it happen that the patient, who now knew about his traumatic experience, nevertheless behaved as if he knew no more than before?" (Sigmund Freud, *Collected Works IV*, 475)

3. While some people may object to the use of the word "trance" because of its association with various kinds of quackery, it is in fact the best word to describe what occurs in the progress of a successful life history. Therefore I will utilize the term rather than create a new name for this phantasy state. An essential condition of therapeutic transformation is therefore properly designated by the term "trance."

4. Jurgen Habermas, *Knowledge and Human Interests*, Boston: Beacon Press, 1971, pp. 264-269.

5. Elizabeth Wappelshammer and Therese Weber, *Auch Lebensgeschichte ist Geschichte* (tr. *Life History Is History, Too*), Vienna, 1985, p. 16.

Grandparenthood, Life Review, and Psychosocial Development

Helen Q. Kivnick

LIFE REVIEW

In his seminal discussion of life review, Butler (1963) discussed this phenomenon as ". . . a naturally occurring, universal mental process characterized by the progressive return to consciousness of past experiences, and, particularly, the resurgence of unresolved conflicts" (p. 66). Attempting to explain the reminiscing often observed in the aged, he proposed life review as a mechanism activated by an awareness of impending death and facilitating the individual's constructive preparation for this final transition. Earlier-life conflicts and failures return, unbidden, from the realm of the forgotten. The elder is then able to re-evaluate them as components of a whole life lived and to accept them as unalterable. In so doing, he or she may be expected to undergo a measure of healthy personality reorganization.

Kaminsky (1984) credits Erikson with providing the theoretical context for this process of life review, explaining that "Erikson views the great task of the final stage of life as the integration of all the previous stages of one's life and as the attainment of 'the acceptance of one's one and only life cycle as something that had to be and that, by necessity, permitted of no substitutions'" (p. 147). In turn, Kaminsky continues, Butler has provided a clear explanation of the process whereby the elder struggles to achieve the ego integ-

---

Helen Q. Kivnick is an associate of the California School of Professional Psychology, Berkeley, CA, co-author with Eric H. Erikson of *Vital Involvement In Old Age* and author of scholarly articles on grandparenthood.

rity of a successful old age. Reviewing the past makes accessible a lifetime of shifting sands, bringing into focus the brightly colored pebbles and razor-edged shells of experience that have, over the years, lain buried in the dunes. Sifting through these newly revealed old treasures allows the elder to make sense of them as inter-related parts of the whole that has been the one and only life cycle.

PSYCHOSOCIAL DEVELOPMENT

Healthy psychosocial development in later life involves far more than coming to terms with the past and its inalterability. In their recent elaboration of life-cycle theory, Erikson, Erikson, and Kivnick (1986) refute the oversimplified image of each psychosocial task as a definitive battle between a syntonic and a dystonic tendency, for example, between integrity and despair. This erroneous battle image portrays one tendency as defeating the other. Victory for the syntonic tendency implies psychosocial success, victory for the dystonic, failure. More accurate, however, is the image of a balance in whose pans syntonic and dystonic tendencies shift toward equilibrium. It would be ludicrous to expect any aging individual's sense of integrity to banish all feelings of despair. Today's life is too full of the unpredictable and the uncontrollable; yesterday's life contains too many irremediable mistakes. Reciprocally, it is not that the overly fearful and despairing elder is wholly without acceptance of the personal past. Rather, the elder is involved in a struggle to bring feelings of integrity and acceptance into some kind of balance with realistic fears and desperations. The precise natures of syntonic and dystonic, of the individual's senses of integrity and of despair, change with each day's thoughts, feelings, memories, and experiences. Thus, an equilibrium is never reached, once and for all. Instead, the elder engages in a continuous, ongoing process of integration, seeking somehow to acknowledge all of life's experiences and emotions, and to bring them into some kind of dynamic balance.

Erikson, Erikson, and Kivnick also refute the rigid notion that a psychosocial stage or task is wholly defined by the parameters of the opposing tendencies that dominate it. On the familiar life-cycle chart presented in Figure 1, this overly limited view implies that

FIGURE 1

PSYCHOSOCIAL STAGES OF LIFE

Old Age								Integrity vs. Despair. WISDOM
Adulthood							Generativity vs. Self-absorption. CARE	
Young Adulthood						Intimacy vs. Isolation. LOVE		
Adolescence					Identity vs. Confusion. FIDELITY			
School Age				Industry vs. Inferiority. COMPETENCE				
Play Age			Initiative vs. Guilt. PURPOSE					
Early Childhood		Autonomy vs. Shame, Doubt. WILL						
Infancy	Basic Trust vs. Basic Mistrust. HOPE							

development takes place only in those boxes that march up the diagonal from lower left to upper right, and, perhaps, that we might eliminate the rest of the chart altogether. However it is the entire chart and all of its sixty-four boxes that represent the life cycle. For at each stage the individual engages not only the thematic tension that is currently focal. At each stage, the individual is also involved in renewing equilibria reached for tensions that were focal in earlier years; this psychosocial work concerning the past is represented by the boxes above the prominent diagonal. At each stage the individual is also involved in anticipating those tensions that will become focal in the future; these processes are represented by the boxes below the diagonal. Thus in later life, the individual struggles to balance senses of integrity with despair, and as part of this struggle he or she is also involved in rebalancing earlier tensions between generativity and stagnation, intimacy and isolation, identity and confusion, and so on. As the term "integrity" implies, psychosocial development in old age involves the elder in integrating and renewing lifelong senses of hope, will, purpose, competence, fidelity, love, care, and wisdom, each with all of the others.

Finally, recent articulation of life-cycle theory holds that healthy psychosocial development rests on the individual's vital involvement in the diversity of experiences, relationships, institutions, materials, and ideas that constitute the world in which we all live. Balancing any psychosocial tension certainly requires measures of thinking, reflecting, and dreaming. Nonetheless, these and other inner-directed processes are all but meaningless in the absence of the outer-directed processes that vitally involve the individual in the larger world that is life's environment.

In view of these crucial theoretical clarifications, the wisdom that is understood to be the focus of psychosocial development through the long years of old age must comprise far more than "the acceptance of one's one and only life cycle." (Erikson, 1963, p. 268). Along with elements of integrity, of acknowledgement and ownership of the past, wisdom must also comprise elements of despair, of unforgiving rejection of the past and uncalmed fear for the future. Wisdom must incorporate the lifelong strengths of care, love, fidelity, and so on. Wisdom must also rest on the elder's involvement, today, in expressing these strengths in each day's involvements with the world. Generativity and stagnation, for example, are not simply a set of feelings and behaviors demonstrated in an earlier era, and meaningful today as they are re-evaluated in the siftings and sortings of old age. Rather, the balance between them is renewed in the final stage largely as the elder continues to demonstrate these same tendencies in everyday life, today. How does the individual balance expressions of nurturance and concern for others with absorption in personal concerns and the need to secure care from others? How can he or she despair at the inability to undo behavior committed long ago, and go on to do better in the time that remains?

Throughout life the concept of care must be understood to include the individual's activities related to procreativity, creativity, and productivity (Erikson, 1980). However the current paper focuses on the element of procreativity and the lifelong intergenerational relationships that often dominate middle adulthood. During this period of ascribed responsibility for the maintenance of the world (Erikson, 1980), parents work to protect, nurture, and socialize their children. They seek both to optimize the survival of the next generation in its world, and to prepare the next generation for its own responsible stewardship of that world. Through the long process of active parenting, adults demonstrate a wide variety of behaviors related to the dominant psychosocial tension between generativity and stagnation. Thus parenthood is closely related, behaviorally, to that psychosocial theme which is viewed as focal in middle adulthood.

As individuals develop through the period of active parenting and beyond, direct responsibility for the maintenance of the world begins to shift to younger shoulders, making way for the later-life care elsewhere described as postmaintenance generativity (Kivnick, 1985a) and grand-generativity (Kivnick, 1985b). Children grow into adults, assuming responsibility for their own lives and moving on to raise their own children. Through lifelong relations with grown children, aging parents find meaningful opportunities to demonstrate postmaintenance generativity and to review and reconcile the caring expressed in earlier life. However the generational cycle also offers the vast majority of aging parents the subsequent relationship of grandparenthood, providing them additional scope for developing grand-generativity. The grandparent finds him- or herself involved in reviewing aspects of earlier life; in evaluating, accepting, and integrating earlier experience; and in making use of all of these intrapersonal processes in the interpersonal relationships that develop with grandchildren. Thus, as grandparents postmaintenance parents take advantage of the process of life review as an opportunity to integrate feelings and expressions of responsible nurturance—both current and lifelong—with those of less productive self-concern. Reciprocally, active grandparenting stimulates further review which, in turn, continues to facilitate psychosocial integration.

GRANDPARENTHOOD

In earlier reports of a study based on a series of open-ended, life-history interviews conducted with thirty respondents and on a structured questionnaire administered to 286 respondents, Kivnick has discussed five simultaneous dimensions of the meaning that grandparents find in grandparenthood (1982; 1983). Every grandparent is understood to attach some degree of importance to each of the five dimensions. "What it means to be a grandparent" is understood to incorporate all five dimensions of meaning, as follows: (1) Centrality—grandparenthood as central to a grandparent's current, daily life; (2) Valued Elder—passing on tradition, history, and advice; (3) Immortality through Clan—patriarchal or matriarchal responsibility, identification with grandchildren, and family immortality; (4) Reinvolvement with Personal Past—grandparents' re-experiencing their own pasts and identifying with their own grandparents; and (5) Indulgence—grandparental attitudes of leniency, permissiveness, and gratification.

What does grandparenthood meaning have to do with the everyday lives of elder grandparents? Why should these dimensions be of concern to those who are interested in life review and the well-being of the aged? Reconciling integrity with despair in later life, and renewing a sense of caring in balance with self-concern must be related to the satisfaction that is associated with psychosocial well-being at all stages of the life cycle. Those elders who live with vitality and resilience manage to reclaim and rework the personal past in such a way as to permit satisfaction in the present. As grandparents, they find that earlier life contributes to the importance they attach to the various dimensions of meaning, to the behaviors through which they express that importance, and to the satisfaction they experience as a result. By and large, these themes and meanings are not articulated. Rather, the processes of review and reintegration take place apart from conscious scrutiny. When frustration and despair outweigh grandparent satisfaction, however, explicit attention to grandparenthood meaning and behavior and assisted recollection of earlier experience may reactivate the elder's innate capacities for integration and grand-generativity capacities—essential to psychosocial health in old age.

Centrality

For some grandparents, grandparenthood assumes a position of dominance in daily life. The importance of other activities and relationships diminishes in comparison to the gratifications of grandparenting. The weight of other aspects of identity evaporates beside the import of being a grandparent. The meaning of life, itself, is enriched by the existence of grandchildren and the grandparent's love for them. Of the five dimensions of grandparenthood meaning, Centrality would seem to be the one most firmly rooted in the present, and perhaps least dependent on the grandparent's reviewing of earlier life. Indeed, the comments associated with Centrality concern experiences in the present, as grandparents live from day to day. "I like to see my grandchildren more than anything else I can think of." "An important part of grandparenthood is the new level of meaning and fullness it has added to my life." "You always wish for grandchildren." "My grandchildren keep me young." "I am someone whose life revolves around my grandchildren."

But the present in which grandparenthood is so central is, itself, inextricably bound to the past and the elder's new relationship with it. And time spent together with grandchildren, or apart from them and thinking about them, inevitably involves the grandparent in recalling—and reordering—some aspect of the past. One woman who likes to see her grandchildren more than anything else she can think of leads a life of active affinity. She delivers Meals on Wheels. She plays bridge in a longstanding foursome. She attends lectures and films with friends. She volunteers in a local nursing home. She does not break previous commitments when her grandchildren visit. She does not abandon the people and activities of her current life during those periods when she assumes primary responsibility for the grandchildren. But she finds herself thinking about the grandchildren and looking forward to their company while she is doing everything else. When she plays bridge with women she has known for over fifty years, they invariably find themselves recalling the circumstances of early friendship, the period of everyone's early marriage, the years of young motherhood. Together they laugh over embarrassments shared and crises of long ago that, in retrospect, no longer feel so horrible. Alongside these reminiscences of a lifetime, however, are her feelings of satisfaction engendered by the grandchildren today.

She explains, "In my mind's eye, I can see them smiling at me every minute of the day. No matter what I'm doing or who I'm talking to, one of them is always right there with me." These images become part of this grandmother's process of life review, as they are part of everything else she does. The past experiences she relives are integrated into a present that includes the special feelings borne of grandparenthood. When she conquers old frustrations, this new mastery carries the special strength she feels as a grandmother. Old memories are brought forth by a woman who defines herself as a grandmother, and their images are juxtaposed with images of the grandchildren who contribute so much to the resilience she feels today.

Grandparenthood also makes a different kind of contribution to her life review. This woman is now in her 70s, and her grandchildren range in age from just under ten to well over twenty. The grandmother role has been part of her life for over twenty years. Since her mid-50s. Since before her husband retired and died. Since before her son was divorced and her sister took sick. The grandchildren and her identity as a grandmother are part of these last two decades and the losses they have brought her. They are part of the memories she summons from these years, illustrating the mix of joy and pain she believes God has apportioned for each of His children. Their enduring presence in her recollections of the recent past gives her a reassuring sense of continuity, in the face of the losses and disruptions she struggles to master. Their presence today allows her to continue to experience the satisfaction and nurturance she has always regarded as her most salient characteristics.

Valued Elder

Some grandparents view themselves as advisors and emissaries from another era. Theirs is the responsibility of teaching the grandchildren about social and cultural history. It is their role to transmit family history and to acquaint the grandchildren with old family traditions. They view themselves as the grandchildren's connection to history, as the crucial link between the family's youngest generations and those older generations that are no longer represented among the living. As the grandparent transmits advice and history to grandchildren so he or she receives a critically important sense of respect from the grandchildren in return. This dimension includes the grandparent's wish to be remembered after death, with fondness and veneration for wisdom imparted during life.

Valued Elder is closely related to the grandparent's review of past life, for it is the wisdom distilled from a lifetime that constitutes the legacy transmitted to the grandchildren. Grandparents who emphasize this dimension observe, "I want to be part of my grandchildren's memories of their childhood years," "I value passing on cultural traditions to my grandchildren," and "I value being able to teach things to my grandchildren." An inner-directed view of later-life integrity would have grandparents simply recall past wisdom and own it, at the end of life, with dignity and pride. In addition, the Valued Elder dimension encourages the grandparent to look outward. Behavior in this dimension represents the grandparent's reviewing earlier life, and then using the product of that review to serve the interpersonal present and the generational future.

One grandfather particularly values passing on cultural traditions to his grandchildren. An investor well into his 80s, he comes from a family of wealthy Jewish merchants. He was raised among the East Coast Protestant aristocracy at whose hands his parents perpetually sought—and never fully achieved—social acceptance. His first wife was a pianist, his second a painter; he has been widowed for at least ten years. His own financial fortunes fell somewhat short of his forebears', and he laughs when he admits that his children and grandchildren are "no better off than the middle class my father held in such contempt. But they're all a good deal happier. My three girls married hardworking men who had no interest in joining me in business. WASPs, every one. So my grandchildren make their own beds and help with the dishes, as I never did. And without me they wouldn't know the first thing about the family they come from."

He is acutely aware that he can offer his grandchildren a personal connection with an historical era and a social stratum that will otherwise be wholly foreign to them. He is also aware that since his daughters are living lives quite different from the ones their grandfather might have chosen for them, parts of his own grandchildren's heritage will probably be lost unless he provides it. Although he was never a religious Jew, when his grandsons reached adolescence he began to talk with them, each year, about the Jewish holidays they did not celebrate, and about the Jewish people of whom they were so unwittingly a part. He has also enjoyed telling them stories of the estates and servants and glittering opulence of his childhood—that might so easily have been a part of theirs. And he makes a point of taking them to concerts and museums, training their esthetic sensibilities in a way he believes should transcend socioeconomic station.

This man is by no means wholly sanguine about the fragments he accepted and rejected for himself, from his family's cultural heritage. He is pleased that he chose human relationship over the status and convenience associated with servants. He is pleased that he learned the value of discipline, rather than relying on inherited privilege as many of his childhood friends were encouraged to do. Looking at his daughters' financial situations, he wonders if he renounced more of the family wealth and position than necessary. And he is both ashamed and regretful of having rejected the Jewish rituals of his childhood, associated with his grandparents. In old age he is struggling to accept the choices he made for his own life, and those he made in raising his daughters. As he does so he finds himself making informed choices about what he must be sure to bequeath to the grandchildren.

A grandmother in her late eighties has very different ideas about what she as an elder can offer her grandchildren. This woman is a descendant of a hardworking pioneer family that crossed the plains in a covered wagon. With resourcefulness, perseverance, and ingenuity she raised five difficult children and, on her husband's meager salary, provided esthetic stimulation and reliable support for academic achievement. In what she perceives as the decadent self-indulgence of the 1980s, this grandmother regards it as her responsibility to remind the grandchildren of the tough pioneer stock from which they come. She and her husband have not achieved the success of their early dreams, and as she reviews her own life, attempting to make peace with perceived personal failures, she mines what she regards as the nuggets of wisdom and strength that validate her life, nonetheless. These are her legacy to the grandchildren. She has enjoyed teaching them to garden and to make things with their hands. And she wants them to carry on the value she places on hard work and on the subordination of material pleasure for the sake of family care and solidarity. Particularly this last value is quite alien to them, and the grandmother is saddened to hear her favorite granddaughter assert that having children will depend on whether she can afford to hire a nanny.

This old woman wants very much to be cherished. She knows that she will probably die soon, and she wants to be remembered with the fondness and respect she holds for her own grandmothers. So she no longer tells to the grandchildren the things she most wants them to hear. She knows the grandchildren disagree with her advice and regard her life's experience as irrelevant to them. She has no wish to court their animosity. Although she knows she is withholding what she has that is truly most precious for her grandchildren, she now remains all but silent in their presence for fear of endangering the enduring warmth and respect she hopes they will carry for her forever.

Immortality Through Clan

Some elders view grandparenthood as a source of immortality achieved through the grandchildren who will maintain family continuity into the indefinite future. They assume a patriarchal or matriarchal position in the family, and they accept some measure of responsibility for subsequent generations. They strongly identify with family names and family-wide traditions, and they identify with the grandchildren as generational extensions of themselves and as guardians of family survival.

Like Centrality, this dimension of grandparenthood meaning would seem to have little to do with life review and its focus on the past. Rather than facing back, Immortality through Clan is tied to the future, and it concerns the grandparent's fears and hopes about what lies ahead. Emphasis on this dimension prompts the following observations. "As a grandparent it's important to me that my opinion influence other people in the family," and "One way I think about my grandchildren is to think that a part of me will keep living after I, myself, have died."

This dimension paradoxically involves both active influence on and responsibility for grandchildren, and, simultaneously, a passive identification with grandchildren that relieves the grandparent of the need for taking any action whatsoever. The same tension between the need for and the futility of action attends the psychosocial challenge that dominates the end of life. What, if any, are the behaviors that can, today, repair mistakes made decades ago? What are the actions that might ensure eternal serenity? In the face of certain personal mortality, what old-age expressions of care can protect the survival of the generational family? This final challenge may be summarized as coming to terms with the personal past in order to do better in the present and to prepare for the unknowable future that looms beyond death's inevitability. It is the role of life review to facilitate reconciling the past in preparation for the future. In so doing life review must somehow inform the dimension of grandparenthood meaning that anticipates that same future.

Says one grandmother, "I measure out the rest of my life in terms of milestones in the grandchildren's lives. You know, like I'd like to live to see this one married, to see that one graduate, to see this other one have a child." This woman was the oldest daughter in a large Irish Catholic family. Although she is already the grandmother of seven, her own youngest child is just about to enter high school. Never in her life has money been plentiful; always she has had to struggle to see to it that all mouths are fed, that all feet are shod. She has spent her life actively mothering, providing physical sustenance and moral guidance for the young ones entrusted to her care. The importance she attaches to Immortality through Clan is an extension of this lifelong concern. When she pages through family albums she finds herself moving forward and back in time. At a snapshot of her oldest son in his crib, she recalls details about his birth—the color of the day, the unseasonal chill that sent her husband scurrying to light the furnace, only to discover that they were out of oil. Then she moves, seamlessly, to more recent memories about the birth of *his* first child, and to speculations about the family this granddaughter will raise someday.

In recalling her own lifelong experiences around nurturance this grandmother experiences pride in her success in the role she had always been trained to play. In recounting her children's successes, she is again validating her own parenting effectiveness. She provided for their survival; she gave them the support and transmitted the values that have allowed them to hold down good jobs and to maintain strong marriages. In anticipating immortality through the grandchildren, she is once again confirming the values of her past. She has played her assigned active role in the generational cycle. Now it is her privilege to experience vicarious satisfaction through the lives of those whose existence she has made possible.

For a wealthy financier Immortality through Clan has a different connection to the past. This man talks about financial empires and family trees. He discusses marriages in terms of uniting fortunes and consolidating interests. Not a day goes by that he does not recall the forebears whose social position and economic affluence he assumed with such pride and diligence, now nearly seven decades ago. As they trained him and inducted him into the world of men of money, so he has trained and inducted his grandchildren. He regards it as his responsibility to ensure their economic security. And he takes for granted that they will steward his name and his values into the infinite future, as he stewarded those of his grandfather. Indeed, he entrusts his grandchildren not only with his own immortality, but with that of his grandparents and his memories of them, as well.

Reinvolvement with Personal Past

For some grandparents, the most meaningful dimension of this role is the way it allows them to review aspects of earlier life. Sometimes they find themselves thinking back to their own grandchildhoods, remembering grandparents and re-experiencing "the rustle of Grandmother's dress," "the smell of the sea from their house on the Cape where I spent every summer," or "the feel of her lap and the sound of her voice when she read me stories." They muse, "Being a grandparent has made me think about my own grandparents," and "It's important to me to try to emulate my grandparents, to walk in their footsteps." At other times they find themselves remembering their own earlier adulthoods, recalling first-time parenthood, for example, when their first child gives birth to their first grandchild.

Of all of the dimensions of grandparenthood meaning, Reinvolvement with Personal Past is most clearly and most closely tied to the process of life review. By definition, this is the dimension through which elders explicitly link contemporary grandparenthood with the earlier experiences. Some individuals describe playing with grandchildren and unexpectedly finding themselves thinking of earlier times and other faces. A grandmother tells of helping her granddaughter memorize a poem for school recitation, and suddenly remembering an incident she hadn't thought of for perhaps sixty years—of walking into the woods as a schoolgirl and reciting poetry to the trees and rocks, who would not ridicule as her brothers surely would. "That made me think a little harder about why she chose me to help with her poem. First I'd thought it was just because I had the time, and of course she knows I love to see her. But then I thought maybe she was being smarter than I'd given her credit for. 'Cause she somehow knew I wouldn't laugh, and that when she got it right I'd really enjoy the recitation."

Grandparents often find themselves flooded with personal memories at night, as they think back over the day's adventures with the grandchildren. A grandmother recounts her experience of taking two grandchildren to the museum. "They nearly ran me nuts! They were just waltzing through the rooms of the museum—you know, there's a kind of library hush in a museum. And they would come back dancing, you know in high spirits. 'Oh, we've seen this, Nona!' in very loud tones. And then on to the next one, and so on through the whole exhibition.'' This grandmother is a formal woman whose every move is governed by an impeccable sense of propriety. Her mahogany furniture is polished shiny as a mirror. Every surface is decorated with a lace doily. Even her kitchen aprons are starched and spotless. She was more annoyed than amused at her grandchildren's lack of museum etiquette, and although she laughed at the image of two high-spirited children shattering public decorum, she concluded her story by saying that she would never take the two of them anywhere like that again. She went on to wonder why her son wasn't training his children more conscientiously. After all, *her* parents and grandparents would never have tolerated such nonsense. She told several stories of her own propriety as a child, suddenly interrupting herself with a long-forgotten memory of kicking up her heels in her grandparents' somber apartment and calling, ''Cabaret! Cabaret!''

Such childhood recollections often prompt grandparents to emulate their own grandparents in their behavior with grandchildren. Quite consciously they decide to try to recreate for their grandchildren, today, the kinds of experiences they remember so warmly from their own grandchildhoods. ''A lullaby from Grandma was something special.'' ''On my birthday they would take me out on the town. The two of them and me, without my parents and without my brother and sisters. They made me feel so special.'' ''To this day I remember the smell of the salami where my grandfather used to take me for lunch.'' ''Granddad took me fishing, and that's where I learned how to fish. We didn't talk all day long. Just sat there, us men together. We'd talk a blue streak on the way home, though. And if we stayed overnight, we'd cook like we'd never do at home. I take my own grandsons fishing now. Each one of them. I want to make sure I do right by them, like Granddad did for me.'' Through this process of emulation, grandparents consciously repeat bits of the personal past as expressions of caring in the present, with an eye to the future. Of course such emulation takes place outside of conscious awareness, as well.

Grandparenthood seems to offer many individuals a ''second chance'' at generativity. Although becoming a grandparent clearly evokes memories of grandchildhood, for many grandparents it also rekindles thoughts of their own active parenthood. And—perhaps because is it too close in time to have fallen into place, perhaps because it is too important for its memories to have been effectively altered—for some people this period is recalled with shame, with guilt, and with regret. A father was too distant. He worked too hard and saw his children too little. A mother was too strict or too demanding. She was not demonstrative enough. The children never felt enough love or appreciation. The parents were preoccupied with themselves. Husband and wife quarrelled too much. They took out on the children their resentments toward each other.

One grandmother recalls having been overinvolved in every aspect of her children's lives. Her children were extraordinarily gifted, and she relentlessly demanded excellence from them in every endeavor. Tension permeated the household, as she remained unsatisfied with the children's levels of achievement and they came to sabotage their own efforts in rebellion against her. In contrast, relations with her grandchildren are warm, relaxed, and mutually respectful. She does not impose expectations on them; she is able to appreciate the accomplishments that give them pride. In her, grandparenthood has elicited or permitted a concerned, respectful nurturance of which she seemed almost incapable as a mother.

The kinds of caring that are called for in grandparenthood are different from those required in parenthood. Primary responsibility is gone; time together is usually spent in short, concentrated periods. By the time they reach grandparenthood, people have had more time to learn to care and nurture, and they have had more practice than they had had when they became parents. For all of these reasons, grandparents can often take advantage of this new role as an opportunity to develop capacities for caring and concern that earlier life simply did not permit. This process of personal remediation illustrates the possibility for renewal and the necessity for vital involvement described at the outset of this paper. Looking inward, these grandparents relive what they experience as the parental failings of earlier life. With this same inward gaze, they struggle to accept past failings as somehow necessary at the time and, in any case, inalterable from the present. But these grandparents are managing to transcend the inward focus of life review, turning it outward to influence the way they live today. They are reworking earlier, inadequate balances between generativity and stagnation. As grandparents they are demonstrating care far more comprehensively than they did as parents. In developing new strengths, they are also making it easier for themselves to accept earlier weakness.

Indulgence

Almost every grandparent delights in the opportunity to "spoil" the grandchildren – to be lenient, indulgent, frivolous, and tolerant as they never could be as parents. This indulgence is tied to grandparents' recollections of the past in a variety of ways. As noted earlier, some grandparents treasure memories of having been indulged as grandchildren, and they are eager to do the same for their own grandchildren. Many of them admit that they have been praying, for decades, to have grandchildren, and to be healthy and wealthy enough to carry out the various adventures they have been remembering since childhood. Some respondents grew up without ever knowing grandparents. Others, though very few, remember their grandparents as cruel, angry, or withholding. These people are eager to treat their grandchildren with kindness and generosity. For them, this is life's first opportunity to participate actively in a relationship about whose joys they have, until now, seen and heard only from the outside.

It is the earlier life of parenthood that indulging grandparents most often recall. They think back to the strained finances, the worries for the future, and the daily challenges that constituted those days and years. Conscious of their responsibility, they were concerned with raising their children well, with providing the support and instilling the values that would allow the children to become independent, successful adults. Even in periods of prosperity they worried about spoiling the children and, in so doing, failing to discharge their parental duty. For these people, grandparenthood's freedom from responsibility allows them to demonstrate unrestrained affection, to give lavish gifts, to express nonjudgmental support with a clear conscience. Discipline is now the responsibility of the grandchildren's parents; these elders need no longer rein themselves in. They need no longer endure a child's fury at discipline or restriction implemented "for his own good." Their memories are full of such incidents and of doubts about whether they were doing the right thing after all. "If I were really being a good mother," they wonder, "would he be so unhappy? Would he get so angry with me?"

Now, at last, the grandparents are free. They may break small rules; they may giggle at serious moments. They are free to give; they are free to sympathize and to understand. They are also free to enjoy. As these people recall earlier adulthood, many of them share surprisingly few memories of happiness. They remember pain and problems, and they remember warmth, love, and satisfaction. But it is almost as if they could not allow themselves to experience unmitigated joy without somehow violating parental responsibility. Now those direct responsibilities for the maintenance of the world no longer rest with them. As grandparents, they are free to indulge their grandchildren as they were never free to indulge their children. In addition, they are also free to indulge themselves. They are using old age to review the past and re-equilibrate personal strengths and weaknesses, and they are finding themselves newly free to appreciate the pleasures and satisfactions of the present. As grandparents they are, at last, indulging themselves in the priceless joys and wonders of the generational cycle.

REFERENCES

Butler, R, (1963). The life review: An interpretation of reminiscence in the aged. *Psychiatry*, *26*, 65-76.

Erikson, E. H. (1980). On the generational cycle: An address. *International Journal of Psychoanalysis*, *61*, 213-233.

Erikson, E. H. (1963). *Childhood and society* (2nd ed.). New York: W. W. Norton.

Erikson, E. H., Erikson, J. M., & Kivnick, H. Q. (1986). *Vital involvement on old age*. New York: W. W. Norton.

Kaminsky, M. (1984). The uses of reminiscence: A discussion of the formative literature. In M. Kaminsky (Ed.), *The uses of reminiscence: New ways of working with older adults* (pp. 137-156). New York: The Haworth Press.

Kivnick, H. Q. (1985a). Intergenerational relations: Personal meaning in the life cycle. In J. A. Mescham (Ed.), *Contributions to human development: Vol. 14. Family and individual development* (pp. 93-109). Basel, Switzerland: Karger.

Kivnick, H. Q. (1985b). Grand-generativity: Elder's relationships with adult children. In J. Thomas (Chair), *Social networks in adult development*. Symposium conducted at the meeting of Gerontological Society of America, New Orleans.

Kivnick, H. Q. (1983). Dimensions of grandparenthood meaning: Deductive conceptualization and empirical derivation. *Journal of Personality and Social Psychology*, *44*, 1056-1068.

Kivnick, H. Q. (1982). Grandparenthood: An overview of meaning and mental health. *The Gerontologist*, *22*, 59-66.

Late Life Divorce and the Life Review

Helen R. Weingarten

THEORETICAL BACKGROUND

Divorce at any age presents significant challenges to coping and adaptation. Research studies of the general population have amassed considerable evidence linking divorce to disruption not only of one's marital relationship but also of one's relationships with children, extended kin, friends, and community associates (Bohannan, 1971; Weiss, 1975; Weingarten 1985, 1986). Although few empirical studies focusing on later life divorce exist, a body of literature is beginning to develop which suggests that the task of coping with divorce in later life may be distinctively problematic because divorce-associated life changes occur in conjunction with additional stressful life changes that are inextricably intertwined with the normative process of growing older—retirement, the deaths of aging friends and colleagues, dwindling physical powers, and so forth (Chiriboga, 1979; DeShane & Wilson, 1981; Hagestad, Smyer, & Steirman, 1984; Hennon, 1983; Lloyd & Zick, 1986; Troll, Miller & Atchley, 1979; Uhlenberg & Myers, 1981).

Robert Butler has suggested that, for the older person, these normative changes in and of themselves trigger the ". . . universal occurrence of an inner experience or mental process of reviewing one's life. . . . " (1963, p. 265). This "life review" experience, he

---

Helen R. Weingarten is Associate Professor of Social Work and Co-Director of the Program on Conflict Management Alternatives at the University of Michigan. She is the author of numerous studies of divorce throughout the life cycle.

The author wishes to acknowledge Robert Disch, Ritsuko Greene, Ellen Whipple-Nickloloff and the members of "Divorce-After-Sixty" for their help in making this publication possible.

has argued, not only promotes the evolution of such characteristics as candor and wisdom among the aged but, if unsuccessfully resolved, may also be a prime contributor to the prevalence of later life symptomatology. Divorce researchers such as Robert Weiss (1975) have presented similar arguments positing that a critical factor in post-divorce adjustment is whether the person can develop an ego-syntonic and meaningful account of the divorce through a life review process.

To Weiss and other social constructionist theorists (e.g., Berger & Kellener, 1964; Vaughn, 1983; Weigart & Hastings, 1980), the negative impact of divorce does not solely result from the loss of significant attachments and roles. Rather, its painful and disruptive effects are exacerbated by the fact that in contemporary America, attachment and meaning have become localized in only one institutionalized relationship—marriage. Thus, while it is possible for the social construction of a meaningful reality to take place in social relationships other than the conjugal one, to the extent that the nuclear family has become more and more segregated from the immediate controls and supports of other institutions (Skolnick, 1979), both the importance of the marital relationship as a source of meaning and identity bestowal and the potential for it to fail in fulfilling this function have grown.

The works of both Butler and Weiss imply that the process of life review should be particularly relevant to the adjustment of those who divorce in later life. Both theories suggest that positive divorce outcomes will be associated with a process of life review that permits the person to experience him or herself as having integrity despite the loss of the particular marital relationship whereas negative outcomes will emerge when one's sense of personal integrity remains tied to the lost marital role. Furthermore, although the nature of such influence remains to be empirically specified, both theories suggest that the relationship between reviewing one's life and divorce outcomes is likely to vary from one situation to another. For example, while in one instance a dissatisfied partner might decide to seek divorce as a result of a life review experience, in another, an unsolicited divorce might initiate and shape the life review process itself.

THE STUDY

A study was designed to broaden our understanding of later life divorce and to clarify factors which appear to facilitate or hamper adjusting to and coping with divorce among older individuals. It is important to study divorce among older persons because, although divorce is an increasingly prominent feature of the social life of mature Americans, our empirical knowledge of its impact among this population group is almost totally lacking (Lloyd & Zick, 1986). Indeed, while the rate of divorce among younger cohorts has begun to stabilize over the past decade, the rate of divorce increased 50% among persons between the ages of 40 and 65 and 35% among persons 65 and older (Thornton & Freedman, 1983).

The Sample

During the four year study period, 121 couples in which one or both partners were at least 60 years old at the time of filing, petitioned for divorce in Washtenaw County, Michigan. This paper reports and comments on the results of: (a) repeated observations of and discussions with approximately 40 women and 3 men from this population as they participated in meetings of a peer-initiated and organized self-help group—"Divorce-After-Sixty"; and (b) intensive, open-ended (2 to 10 hours), individual research interviews with 12 women and 2 men from the group and 3 women and 3 men, who although not associated with "Divorce-After-Sixty," resided locally and met group membership criteria.

With a median age of 65, most of the study participants were dealing with the termination of marriages of 30 to 50 years duration, although a few married late or more than once: Since the group's inception in 1982, approximately 60 women and a handful of men (representing 25% of the couples who filed for divorce in Washtenaw County during the study period) attended "Divorce-After-Sixty" meetings. Most of the meetings consisted, however, of 6 to 10 participants, 4 or 5 of whom formed the working nucleus while others came and went as their needs and others activities dictated.

Gathering the Data Through Participant Observation

My attendance at the meetings of "Divorce-After-Sixty" spanned a four year period from 1983 to 1987 and was initiated at the request of group members. During the course of my involvement in this project, participants were observed and interviewed in both group and individual contexts. Although all individual interview participants were requested to fill out a coping inventory developed at the Center for the Study of Neurosis at the University of California at San Francisco (Horowitz & Wilner, 1980), the primary research method was qualitative and involved listening to and watching as the group process unfolded, asking occasional questions to explore particular issues in more depth, and encouraging respondents interviewed individually to express themselves fully about their personal experience.

A qualitative method of research was chosen because it seemed suited to this early stage in the development of our knowledge about later life divorce. Rather than attempting to link particular behaviors to particular causes, rather than stressing parsimony or prediction, description that could enlarge our perspective and understanding was focused upon. Thus, while recognizing that the convenience nature of the sample and the willingness of the group members to be interviewed placed limits on generalizing from their experience to others, such an approach permitted the discovery of patterns and the raising of questions that could foster more informed and representative research in future.

Results and Discussion

What influences older persons, often married for three decades or more, to end their marriage? Do persons who initiate late life divorces identify a life review process such as Butler describes—

> . . . a naturally-occurring universal mental process characterized by progressive return to consciousness of past experiences, and particularly, the resurgence of unresolved conflicts; simultaneously, and normally, these revived experiences and conflicts are surveyed and reintegrated. (1963, p. 266)

—as being a contributor to their decision to divorce? Or, is a divorce more likely to be initiated by those who, rather than realizing their own "approaching dissolution and death," are looking forward to a changeable and better future? In addition, once the divorce process is underway, what is the relationship between self-reflective life review and coping and adaption?

A complexity in the study of late life divorce is that for some people the commencement of marital dissolution is primarily viewed as a negative life event, whereas for others, at least initially, it is viewed positively. Consequently, no simple relationships among the life review process, divorce initiation, and coping with the effects of divorce were anticipated. It was expected, however, that among those persons who experienced divorce, those who initiated the process would spend considerably more time reflecting about the meaning of their lives prior to taking such action and those who felt victimized by spouses' decision to terminate the marriage would engage in life review subsequent to the decision.

Among the study participants, approximately one-third had initiated their divorce and two-thirds had not. Agnes Richardson's story was typical of the women in the sample who initiated a decision to divorce (*Note*: in all case examples, names and identifying details have been modified to preserve confidentiality). After reading about the group in a local newspaper, she began attending "Divorce-After-Sixty" while still married to her husband, Fred. For thirty years she had lived with his taciturn silence, workaholism, and occasional outbursts of emotional and physical violence. Now, with their three children grown and independently established, facing the prospect of more time together because of his imminent retirement, Agnes was consciously seeking to answer whether a life on her own might be more tolerable than continuing in her long troubled marriage.

According to Levinger and Moles (1979), marital dissolution decisions are based not only on evaluations of the satisfactions available within one's current marriage compared to those found outside but also on one's perceptions of the barriers opposing changes in the status quo. While the decision to divorce of many study participants was made in reaction to the discovery of spousal infidelity, group members identified relaxed social norms about divorce and the absence of minor children in the home as two important factors operating against efforts directed towards marital preservation.

Interestingly, none of the study participants identified a life review process such as Butler (1963) describes as related to their decision to divorce. While statements made in the group ("That's the straw that broke the camel's back" and "I realized she was never going to change") implied that some kind of selective life review had influenced some of the decisions in the divorce process, the participants did not discuss past events in any detail or assign importance to life review strategies in their responses to the coping inventory.

In this group it was not life review but a changing social climate that was reported as influential for those group members whose decision to seek divorce was not based on the infidelity of their partners: Television shows such as "The Golden Girls," the example of a Dr. Spock who leaves a marriage of 48 years to begin a new family life without any obvious negative repercussions seemed to provide public images that allowed the idea of leaving an unsatisfying marriage in late life to seem both attractive and plausible.

In addition, both women and men reported that their ongoing relationship with their children, although no longer a powerful barrier against divorce, was one of the most important influences in their decision making. The discovery that her married son not only sympathized with her desire to live apart from his alcoholic father but also encouraged her to move closer to his family was a powerful incentive for Dolores Branch to put an idea she had considered for years into practice. A wife's refusal to allow his daughter and grandchild to move into their home following their daughter's divorce was seen by Melvin Houghton as the straw that broke the camel's back of his own sixteen-year-long second marriage. And for Irene O'Connell, the one respondent to remarry her former husband during the study period, her adult children's refusal to acknowledge their father's new relationship and include him and his "girlfriend" in their family gatherings was seen as the most critical factor leading the couple to reconcile after a two year estrangement.

The decisional processes leading to late life divorce for men and for women do not always appear similar, however. Although both men and women report dissatisfaction with their spouse as the prime determinant of their decision to divorce, gender differences emerged in the nature of the dissatisfactions cited. For example, in the sample interviewed, men were likelier than women to view their estranged partners as too critical or unable to share activities and interests they currently wanted to pursue (e.g., "Around her I feel old; all she wanted to do was spend time with family. I'm still young. I want to travel and make new friends"). In addition, dissatisfied men not only wanted to be with someone who shared their interests, they seemed to want their interests to come first. In contrast, women were more likely to complain about their partner's refusal to communicate and offer emotional or instrumental support (e.g., "We never talked. Even when our daughter died, I was left to make all the funeral arrangements. I felt isolated.") When dissatisfactions were expressed by women they had more to do with a husband's long-term failures to provide support rather than with current refusals to initiate or share new patterns of behavior.

That retirement serves to initiate an especially significant and identity relevant role loss for men may help explain why the need to have his interests come first seems so salient for the man who initiates a divorce after age 60 but not for the woman. It is also interesting to note that Lowenthal, Thurner, and Chiriboga (1975), in a study examining values of different age cohorts, found achievement values prevalent in younger groups of men whereas more hedonistically oriented values were normative for the older male cohort. Although they also found no evidence of a similar trend for women, because the sample participating in this study of late life divorce had so few men in it, no conclusions about whether hedonistic values are more prevalent among divorcing men than women during the sixth decade should be drawn at this time.

When we move from considering the reasons people offer for leaving long term marriages to the factors that enable them to cope with that reality, the importance of finding ways to carry out the ethic of care and responsibility remains a central concern for the older divorced women. Numerous studies have emphasized the importance of maintaining a positive sense of identity as a key factor in post-divorce adjustment (Weingarten, 1981; Weiss, 1975). Anthropologist Paul Bohannan (1971) in theorizing that most divorcing individuals will experience identity problems, argued that the critical identity challenge posed by divorce is resolved when the divorced person recognizes that he or she is an autonomous individual who can exist successfully without the former spouse. However, in this study of persons divorced after age sixty, rather than autonomy being the critical dimension around which identity is forged, feeling "needed" and "affirmed" seemed to have particular relevance for post-divorce adjustment.

Erik Erikson's (1963) identification of "generativity" as an especially salient motive in later life gained support from our respondents when it was observed that they began to speak well of themselves only after reporting they had found or sought out a situation in which they could be helpful to others. As one respondent answered when asked "What do you think it would take for you to feel happier now?"

> I have thought about how I want to change my life. Now 15 years ago, I was busy all the time, I had ten or fifteen things going. I was making hats; I made all my own clothes except for shoes—I never have made a pair of shoes. I knitted. I did woodwork. I had a lathe. I made jewelry from stones and sold a lot of them. . . . I was helping my children with things. . . . and right now I don't feel like I'm making much of a contribution to society. I'm just here. I think what I need is to feel that I'm really making a difference by being alive and being here, that I'm not just taking up space.

For some, helping others entailed increasing their involvements with church, workplace, or volunteer organizations such as "Divorce-After-Sixty" itself. For others, these involvements centered on adult children and grandchildren. Yet regardless of the arena chosen, the quality of participation allowed by the situation affected whether it served as a source of identity and meaning, was perceived as worthless in itself, or further undermined confidence and self-regard.

It was very important that older divorced respondents could view their post-divorce contributions to others as a confirmation and affirmation of their established sense of identity. Indeed, as Weiss

(1975) suggests, respondents who were unable to develop an account of their divorce that preserved their sense of being "all right as they were" seemed to "despair" much as Erikson (1963) theorized was likely to occur when the work of ego integration has been disrupted or blocked. However, here too, a Butlerian process of life review was either not mentioned as being germaine to the construction of this "account" or was reported as being less effective than other methods of coping.

As described in the section on methodology, all individual interviewees were asked to respond to a standardized survey asking them about their use and assessment of 33 methods of coping with their divorce (Horowitz & Wilner, 1980). For each item, a respondent could select as applicable one of three categories: (a) Does not apply; (b) Does apply; and (c) Does apply and was very useful. If we look at the items that seem to most closely reflect the process of life review as depicted by Butler, none were identified as useful by the majority who responded. For example, of the eleven respondents who agreed to fill out the questionnaire *none* selected the category "Does apply and was very useful" in response to the statement. "I tried to work out how the event related to things in my past"; only *two* selected that category in response to the statements, "I tried to think through the meanings of the event for my life at present" and "I tried to experience all my feelings and work them through"; and only *three* did so in response to the statements, "I thought about events in my past life which might help me to deal better with the present" and "I tried to figure out why the event evoked the feelings that it did." In contrast, *eight* respondents reported that trying "to find people who had experienced the same kind of event to see how they dealt with it did apply and was very useful and *six* felt that way in response to the statement "I sought increased emotional support from others."

Anger, sadness, pain, feelings of helplessness, and the desire to connect with empathic others were typically reported as feelings that led respondents to seek assistance from people going through a similar life event. Participants in "Divorce-After-Sixty" also believed that talking about the dissolution of their marriage with others in the same situation, helped. It is noteworthy, however, that the conversations that were observed to be most helpful (and thus repeated at meeting after meeting) were not conversations that encouraged participants to look at their own contributions to the breakdown of their marriages or engage in serious self-analysis.

Although newcomers to the group would generally blame themselves as well as their spouses for the failure of their marriages, self-blame was markedly reduced as group participation continued. The interactional sequence that appeared to account for this pattern was that experienced group members, listening to a newcomer's story, would pick up and comment on the wrongdoings of the spouse, often comparing his or her actions to that of their own estranged partners, and greet the parts of the story in which the newcomer blamed his or herself with total silence. As time went on, therefore, it was usual to find self-criticism markedly reduced among those who regularly attended the group while the tendency to blame one's partner for marital failures increased.

Researchers such as Brown (1976) and Weiss (1975) have reported that a positive aspect of marital breakup for younger persons inheres in its motivating them to become aware of and change negative patterns of behavior. For this sample of persons divorcing late in life, however, focus on one's own marital failures often appeared associated with continuing depression and guilt. It seems probable that this difference in willingness to look at the past with a self-critical eye is tied to the fact that the individual's time orientation changes as he or she moves across the lifespan (Neugarten & Gutman, 1968). Younger adults, looking towards the future, tie their sense of self-worth to projected accomplishments and thus may see self-criticism as an ego-syntonic path to improved performance. In contrast, the older person with little time or incentive to establish a new personal identity is better served by opportunities that permit self-affirmation rather than self-criticism. Thus, while blaming one's partner for marital failure and believing oneself to have acted in the only way possible is likely to be a distortion of marital history, insofar as it allowed the older person to preserve integrity and worth, its popularity as a coping strategy among study participants makes intuitive sense (George & Siegler, 1982; Langer, E., 1983; Wortman, 1976).

SUMMARY AND MAJOR CONCLUSIONS

Among a sample of respondents from a late-life divorce self-help group, there was no evidence of life review as a common coping strategy for *either* those initiating divorce or those who experienced divorce at the initiative of their partners, at least as they reported coping styles after the event itself. There is a need for further research to determine whether those actively initiating divorce engage in some non-Butlerian form of self-assessment or life review in the process leading up to the decision to act or to ameliorate the impact after the event.

In this group, life review as a coping or adaptive strategy was clearly *not* encouraged by the members. The group as a whole found it more useful to focus their attention on present and future tasks rather than on self-criticism or rumination about the past.

Since neither of the methodologies used in this study revealed the explicit presence of the life review as a coping mechanism, it is possible that methodological limitations could explain the absence. First, both investigative tools were biased against eliciting this kind of information. Their function was to determine the role of coping mechanisms among recently divorced elderly in a retrospective setting. The group meetings were designed to help the participants find ways to solve problems in the present and to build for the future. The participants therefore did not readily pursue deep analyses of the significance of past events or indulge in self-criticism. When the past did intrude, as indeed it had to at some point, the episode described was often used to typify a long pattern of undesirable behavior on the part of the spouse.

The questionnaire, likewise, was designed to elicit information about *coping* styles in the present, not to ferret out information about the influence of ruminations about the past. Since one-third of the participants had initiated their divorce, we would expect, by hypothesis at least, to find some evidence of life review *prior* to initiation of divorce. But this is not the kind of information that can be picked up easily by retrospective queries about coping styles. Had these same people participated in a different kind of group or in Freudian psychotherapy, the results vis-à-vis the life review might have been considerably different. The phenomenon of late-life reminiscence and life review was originally conceived as taking place in old age under the approach of death. But the efficacy of life review, under these restricted conditions, even if it were well established, need not apply to other disruptive late-life events. In fact, among "young-old" divorcees, it may well be that *avoiding* life review is more adaptive and functional for coping with late-life divorce. As the frequency of late-life divorce increases, this point has major implications for clinical practice in gerontological social work. Although it was expected that a Butlerian life review process would be extremely relevant to coping with late life divorce, this seemed true for the study sample only insofar as its avoidance appeared linked with positive adaptation. Social workers who are likely to find themselves working with increasing numbers of persons divorced late in life are therefore urged to proceed very cautiously in promoting the use of reminiscence rather than instrumental action with such clientele.

Butler himself recognized that "constructive outcomes to the life review process are not invariable" particularly when the "process proceeds in isolation in those who have been deeply affected by . . . notable discontinuities, including such psychosocial disruptions as forced retirement and death of a spouse" (p. 271). That divorce is such a disruption has long been recognized in the professional literature which documents that, unresolved, the crisis of divorce leaves in its wake high rates of physical and mental health symptomatology, depression, and suicide among all age groups. (Bloom, Asher & White, 1978; Carter & Glick, 1976; Gove & Tudor, 1973; Holmes & Rahe, 1967; Pearlin & Johnson, 1977). It was clear from this study that social support was particularly critical for coping and adaptation and that the self-selected sample of persons divorcing after age sixty interviewed here, far from viewing their divorce as a signal of "approaching dissolution and death" viewed it, instead, as a challenge to be mastered so they could continue their vital engagement with life.

From the dynamics of the self-help group observed, there is evidence of reluctance to engage in self-criticism or life-review. But this avoidance may not be explained purely by group processes alone. One further explanation for this avoidance may be tied to the scarcity of remaining time for those who experience late-life divorce. Young adults look toward the future and can use self-criticism as a path to improved performance, whereas for older people, self-affirmation may be needed more than self-criticism: hence, the avoidance of life review. On the other hand the same condition of time scarcity is also found among nursing home residents and others for whom life review is apparently a frequent event. What is the true explanation for its distinctive absence among late-life divorcees?

One hypothesis is that, given the need to rebuild relationships and an active social life (even apart from an improbable remarriage) the activity of self-affirmation rather than self-criticism is simply more functional. If this hypothesis is correct, then life review will prove infrequent regardless of the presence or absence of a self-help group. A second hypothesis is that life review is, to some extent at least, an artifact of the audience. Certain professionals (e.g., psychotherapists, social workers) may listen for life review, look for It, and encourage it, while self-help group members may either ignore it or reject it because it is threatening. Based on the design of this study we have no way of deciding between these two hypotheses. The subject merits further research.

But the unresolved research question conveys a message of great clinical importance to gerontological social workers. Life review is not a prescribed solution for all older people coping with stressful life changes. For some it may be; for others not at all. In a sense, the clinical problem—to encourage life review or not—runs parallel to a broader question coming out of empirical studies of the psychological impact of life review. For some elders, life review seems to improve mental health and life satisfaction; for others, the opposite seems true. Gerontological social workers must exercise clinical judgment and discretion as they balance self-criticism about the past with the demands of living in the present.

REFERENCES

Berger, P. & Kellner, H. (1964). Marriage and the construction reality. *Diogenes*, 46, 1-25.

Bloom, B., Asher, S. & White S. (1978) Marital disruption as a stressor: a review and analysis. *Psychological Bulletin*, 85(4), 867-94.

Bohannon, P. (1971). The six stations of divorce. In Paul Bohannon (Ed.), *Divorce and after*. New York: Anchor Books, 33-62. .

Brown, P. (1976). Psychological distress and personal growth among women coping with marital dissolution. Unpublished doctoral dissertation. University of Michigan, Ann Arbor, MI.

Butler, R. (1963). The life review. An interpretation of reminiscence in the aged, *Psychiatry*, 26, 65-76.

Carter, H. & Glick, P. C. (1976). *Marriage and divorce: A social and economic study*. Cambridge, Mass. Harvard University Press.

Chiriboga, D. A. (1979). Marital separation and stress: A life-course perspective. *Alternative Lifestyles*, 2(4), 461-470.

Deshane, M. R., & Wilson, K. B. (1981). Divorce in late life: A call for research. *Journal of Divorce*, 4(4), 81-91.

Erikson, E. H. (1963). Eight ages of man. In E. H. Erikson, *Childhood and society*. New York: W. W. Norton & Company, 247-274.

George, L. K. & Siegler, I. C. (1982). Stress and coping in later life. *Educational Horizons*, 147-154 ff.

Gove, W. R. & Tudor, J. F. (1973). Adult sex roles and mental illness. *American Journal of Sociology*, 78, 812-835.

Hagestad, G. O., Smyer, M. A., & Steirman, K. L. (1984). The impact of divorce in middle age. In. R. S. Cohen, B. J. Cohler, & S. H. Weirsman (Eds.), *Parenthood: A psychodynamic perspective*. New York: Guilford Press.

Holmes, T. H. & Rahe, R. H. (1967). The social readjustment rating scale. *Journal of Psychosomatic Research*, 11, 213-218.

Horowitz, M. J. & Wilner, N. (1980). Life events, stress and coping. In L. W. Poon (Ed.) *Aging in the 1980's: Psychological issues*, Washington, D.C. American Psychological Association, p. 363-374.

Hennon, C. B. (1983). Divorce and the elderly—A neglected area of research. In T. Brubakez (Ed.). *Family relationships in later life*. pp. 149-172.

Langer, E. (1983). *The psychology of control*. Beverly Hills, CA: Sage.

Levinger, G. & Moles, O. C. (1979). *Divorce and separation*. New York: Basic Books.

Lloyd, S. A. & Zick, C. D. (1986). Divorce at mid and later life: Does the empirical evidence support the theory. *Journal of Divorce*, 9(3), 89-102.

Lowenthal, M. F., Thurner, M. & Chiriboga, D. (1975). *Four stages of life*. San Francisco: Jossey-Bass.

Morris, M. B. (1979). Retirement benefits, divorce and community property. In *Women and retirement income programs: Current issues of equity and adequacy*. (Comm. Pub. No. 96-190). Congressional Research Service of the Library of Congress Washington, D.C. (November 1979), 77-79.

Neugarten, B. L. & Gutmann, D. L. (1968). Age-sex roles and personality in middle age: A thematic apperception study. In B. Neugarten (Ed.) *Middle-age and aging*. Chicago: U. Chicago Press, 58-71.

Pearlin, L. I. & Johnson, J. S. (1977). Marital status, life-strains, and depression. *American Sociological Review*, 42, 704-715.

Skolnick, A. (1979). Public images and private realities. In Tufte, V., & Myeroffi N. (Eds.), *Changing images of the family*. New Haven, CT: Yale University Press.

Stern, N. & Campbell, R. (1983). "Divorce-After-Sixty" paper delivered Group Work Conference, Detroit, MI.

Thornton, A. & Freedman, D. (1983). The changing American family. *Population Bulletin*, 38(4), 1-49.

Troll, L. E., Miller, S. J., & Atchley, R. C. (1979). *Families in later life*. Belmont, CA: Wadsworth.

Uhlenberg, P., & Meyers, M. A. P. (1981). Divorce and the elderly. *The Gerontologist*, 21, 276-182.

Vaughn, D. (1983). Uncoupling: the social construction of divorce. In Robboy, H. & Clark, C. (Eds.) *Social interaction: Readings in sociology, 2nd edition*. New York: St. Martin's Press.

Weigart, A. & Hastings, R. (1980). Identity, loss, family, and social change. *American Journal of Sociology*, 82(6), 1171-1185.

Weingarten, H. (1980). Remarriage and well-being. National survey evidence of social and psychological effects. *Journal of Family Issues*, 1(4), 553-559.

Weingarten, H. (1985). Marital Status and well-being: A national survey comparing first married, divorced, and remarried adults. *Journal of Marriage and the Family*, 47(3), 653-662.

Weingarten, H. (1986). Strategic planning for divorce mediation. Social Work, 31(3), 191-200.

Weiss, R. S. (1975). *Marital separation: Coping with the end of a marriage and the transition to being single again*. New York: Basic Books.

Wortman, C. (1976). Causal attribution and personal control. In J. H. Harvey, W. J. Ickes, & R. F. Kidd (Eds.) *New directions in attribution research*. Hillsdale, NY: Erlbaum, 23-52.

III. ADAPTATIONS AND APPLICATIONS

All That Our Eyes Have Witnessed: Memories of a Living History Workshop in the South Bronx

Marc Kaminsky

> Death is the sanction of everything that a storyteller can tell. He has borrowed his authority from death.
>
> Walter Benjamin
> "The Storyteller"

In 1978, I conducted a Living History Workshop in the South Bronx, in a synagogue that could not afford its own rabbi, or even its heating bill, and so had to rent space to a senior citizens' center. When I was growing up, in a five-story walkup around the corner, it hadn't been a synagogue: it was a branch office of a Metropolitan Life Insurance Company. A ranch-style "taxpayer," the building's single story brought the suburb's spacious way of life home to us, in a kind of jolting and monumental advertisement for the exodus to Westchester that was taking place all around us. After giving up on our neighborhood, the company sold the building to a displaced congregation, which had been putting up in rented halls since the cataclysm of the Cross Bronx Expressway. Within three years, most of the stores on the block were boarded up. The movie theatre

---

Marc Kaminsky, poet and essayist, is founder and director of the Myerhoff Center at the YIVO Institute in New York. His many books include the pioneering *What's Inside You It Shines Out of You, The Uses of Reminiscence: New Ways of Working with Older People* and *Daily Bread*, a book of poems and photographs on aging.

tried showing skin flicks; then it, too, went dark. That was in 1968. Even my grandmother got out.

For nearly forty years, my grandmother Esther had lived two blocks away, in the grandly styled Marjorie Hall. This apartment complex, built just before the First World War, consisted of five connected buildings that enclosed a formal garden with a fountain at the center. It combined the imagery of the medieval walled city, the Jewish ghetto, and the aristocratic pleasure garden that itself reproduced the traditional image of paradise. "The green and pleasant parks of the Bronx"—so read the handbill my grandfather Alter picked up on Delancey Street one day in 1913—became the middle-class idea of the heavenly city that my immigrant grandparents pursued after abandoning, without apparent difficulty, the Messianic hopes of their Orthodox fathers and, a few years later, again without much soul-wrenching, the socialist dream of a redeemed life in a just society. Now, sixty-five years later, less than a mile away, the fires that were razing the refuge they had once found here could be seen, past midnight, from the bedroom and living room windows of the ten old people in the workshop.

Not one of the old people in the group had been born in New York City. Most had come from other countries: Rumania, British Honduras, Puerto Rico, Austria. We discovered, soon enough, the common ground that they shared. Everyone in the group had been born into a rural congregational community. Sarah Zeitlin told us that on Friday evenings she had helped her mother prepare a stew of meat and beans called *cholent*; she had placed the pot at the back of the red-brick oven, to keep the food warm for the Sabbath. On a farm in British Honduras, Brodell Borden had buried the sabbatical stew among burning embers, in a stone-lined pit near the house, from whence it was retrieved for the Sunday dinner. Whether they had been raised in a shtetl in Eastern Europe or on a farm in the mountains of Puerto Rico, *jibaro* or Hasid, they had all learned to take the creases out of their clothes with the same tool: an iron like an upside-down hull whose hollowness they filled with hot coals. As children, they had all prepared for the Sabbath by performing the same tasks: sweeping the yard, carrying water in from the well, tending cows, chickens, and goats. They discovered, in the detailed recollection of actual social practices, that their lives had been shaped by parallel values, parallel traditions and technologies.

And they fell in love: less, perhaps, with each other than with the situation in which the astonishing connections among them were made. The racial tension in the senior center decreased, as an unlooked-for by-product of their "work of remembering." It turned out that the ten members of the workshop constituted the center's Executive Committee. They had been told by the director of the center that it was their privilege and their duty to join this group. The respect, and even affection, they came to feel for each other radiated outward and transformed the tone of the center as a whole.

They discovered, too, that they had more in common than stew and coal-heated irons. Ruth Carter, who grew up in Georgia, recounted the race riots of 1919. She told the story of how her brother saved his life by "shimmying on his belly" through the town—under two blocks of parked cars. A skinny boy of twelve: he "holed up under a Ford" until nightfall, when the houses of Blacks were torched; then he began his long crawl home. Other boys, friends of theirs, never made their way back.

Risa Eistenstadt then told the story of *Kristallnacht*, "the night of glass": November 9, 1938.

> That night fires were set all over Germany, and glass—window glass—and plate glass of shopwindows—everywhere the streets were covered with ruined windows, of synagogues, Jewish homes and newspapers and . . . a whole way of life, in ruins on the ground. Burnt. Destroyed. And this was only the beginning. A hundred Jews were killed that night. Dropped into rivers. Axed. Thirty-thousand men—the first roundup—were arrested and sent to concentration camps. At the time, we thought: such a thing can't be! It's impossible. And later we learned: that was nothing—a drop in the bucket.

We spent the next three Thursdays discussing the hidden and not-so-hidden injuries of racism. We heard bitter tales in which subtle gestures were taken as signs of an institutionalized violence that had been brutal to them, and in which violence was an always-expected event. The "sensitivity" ascribed to these elders by people who had never been directly exposed to race murder, let alone race prejudice, rankled them. Morris Feinberg called it "an insult, it's a way of protecting themselves from what really happened to us." Dave Waldman nodded sadly, "Sometimes from my own children I get this, they just don't want to hear about it. I try to tell about the days you go for a job, over the door it says, "Sheenies and Dogs! Don't apply! But we lived these things, we know . . ."

As we talked, the people in the workshop returned in imagination to sites of loss and reviewed long forgotten implements and symbols and events; they rummaged among stranded objects and reclaimed them. The muteness of experience for which no listener can be found came to an end, in an air of discovery. "Sometimes we have to wait for years," writes Edmond Jabes, "before the moment which marked us finds its voice."[1] For many, not only the transformative moments, but also the ordinary hours of which the past is mostly composed, had fallen in value in their own eyes because of their estrangement from the present, their distance from welcoming attention. Collective remembrance transvalued the past; it became the site where story-telling was a form of spade-work that turned up precious materials.

These were then worked up in autobiographical narratives and poems, and into the graphic images that were intertwined with the text. Each person in the workshop produced a "memory book" that, with its colorful borders and hand-painted cover, with photographs pasted in, and major life-events illustrated in full-page tempera or oil paintings, resembled an illuminated manuscript. No two were alike. Margot Rodriguez had saved the airplane tickets of every trip she had taken, from Puerto Rico to New York and back again. A montage of her life's itinerary was composed of these relics, woven together with contemporaneous photographs of her family. Morris Feinberg created a collage that included a postcard from the War Department, calling him up for service in February, 1917, and a newspaper article about the end of the war; it incorporated the last letter he received from his mother, soon after the war began: the seal that the envelope bore was the Czar's eagle, stamped in red wax.

At a ceremony held one Sunday at the center, the old people handed these books down to their children and grandchildren. Three years later, Dave Waldman called me up to give me the good news that served only to fill him with complaint. It wasn't until his "memory book" was exhibited at Hunter College, and an article appeared in the *Times*, that his son bothered to look into his life story.

The composite form of their books was suggested to me by the *yizker-bikher* ("memorial books") which were collectively created by the survivors of hundreds of destroyed Jewish communities in Europe after the Holocaust. The form of these books arose out of the need that brought them into being. They contained chronicles of vanished communities, portraits of outstanding individuals—rabbis, philanthropists, artists, political leaders—and also of memorable characters—a traveling tailor, a blind cantor, a coachwoman. They included diagrams of former homes, street maps, anecdotes, poems, photographs—nothing that bore witness to the life of the vanished community was excluded. All surviving documents and reminiscences were in-gathered here, since each, as symbol and as information, counteracted the death of dead relatives and neighbors, and of the lost public world the living had shared with the dead.

In their Introduction to *From a Ruined Garden: The Memorial Books of Polish Jewry*, Jack Kugelmass and Jonathan Boyarin write,

> Wherever the dead reside, in some heavenly kingdom or in earthly graves, their presence is felt by the living, and it is through the living that they find a measure of eternal life. Completely overlooked in recent writing about the Holocaust is the single most important act of commemorating the dead on the part of Jewish survivors. These are the hundreds of *yizker-bicker,* memorial books devoted to the lives and deaths of entire Jewish communities in Eastern Europe. . . . The memorial books emerged as a genuinely collective response to the Holocaust. So compelling was the urge to participate in this collective voice that many contributors wrote for the first time in their lives. . . . Why this compulsion to write? Terrence Des Pres has argued convincingly that "the need to bear witness" became a motivating force for many survivors.[2]

The idea of the "memorial book" provided us with a valuable starting point because it gave form to the less catastrophic, though nonetheless real, need many older people feel to battle loss through storytelling, or, as Barbara Myerhoff put it, "to erase the oblivion" that threatens their lives and the remembrance of all that they hold sacred. Then, too, the idea of the *yizker* books made explicit the passion that animated my interest in hearing—and transmitting—stories about the past: my passion for storytelling began as a longing to salvage the vanishing "world of our fathers and mothers." So when the old people asked me, as they always ask at the beginning of a Living History Workshop, "What do you want with us here?" I said my approach to this workshop was lineally descended from Telemachos's approach to the elders of Argos. And I read them this thrice-repeated request, from the pages of the *Odyssey*:

> . . . tell me of his dismal destruction, whether you saw it perhaps with your own eyes, or heard the tale from another who wandered too . . . Do not soften it because you pity me and are sorry for me, but fairly tell me all that your eyes have witnessed. I implore you, if ever noble Odysseus, my father, ever undertook any word or work and fulfilled it for you, in the land of the Trojans where you Achaians suffered, tell me these things from your memory. And tell me the truth.

Our Troy was the South Bronx. Here was our common ground, the final and major connection among us. The social history of every old one in the group included the narrative of a journey that had this place as its terminus: a common migration that had taken them, at some period in their lives, through Harlem. And this was the last in the series of remarkable commonalties that we discovered among them. With one exception, every person in the workshop had lived in Harlem: the Jews more than a half a century ago, when its boundaries included a "Little Russia" as well as a large population of German-Jewish merchants; the Blacks and Puerto Ricans had lived there in the Forties and Fifties. And all of them had moved "up from the ghetto" to this "good neighborhood" in the

Bronx, where they now watched the flames climb up from the valley below Third Avenue, gutting abandoned and tenanted buildings in a steady advance westward.

Returning to the synagogue on Tremont Avenue meant returning to streets where stoops, hydrants and manhole covers were the prisons, safe houses and home plates of my childhood games. I was returning to my own past, to the time and place in which I had commuted between my grandmother's house and my mother's, between Yiddish and English, between the Old World and the New. Back here once again, after an absence of ten years, I experienced the reality of past experience as immediately as the old people, to whom their culture of origin and native ground were vividly restored in a collective effort of historical imagination. For all of us, the burning houses they witnessed each night were a terrible symbol—if it is permissible to speak of this as a symbol—of all that they had fled from, and lived with: the fires of the past were before their eyes, even here, even now.

At our final meeting, Abe Shulman, a survivor of Buchenwald and Mauthausen and Dachau, spoke for the first time about the death camps that had remained, until then, a blank page in his life story. Or rather, four blank pages: one for each of the years he had been "imprisoned"—"altogether too mild a word," he said, "but there is no word for it." "Later," he told the group, "later, I will write the history of those years. I'm still not ready for this." But he considered our meetings part of his lifelong preparation for that task.

He had told us a good deal about his life before the war. He had been an organizer for the Bund, the major Jewish Socialist organization in Eastern Europe. He had played on the Bundist soccer team that had defeated the all-star Polish team in a celebrated match in the Thirties. And we knew of his life starting with his liberation from Dachau by the Russian Army. Like many other survivors, he had taken this day as his birthday. He told us it was raining on the day he was liberated. The Bundist soccer team had survived intact, every last one of them. He passed around a tiny photograph which depicted three rows of athletic young men. The group ooh'ed and aah'ed over Abe's massiveness. And he said that on the third day after their liberation, after lunch, which consisted of a bowl of barley soup and two slices of black bread, this team had challenged the Russians to a game of soccer. He waved his hand before his face, dramatizing the soldiers' response, a gesture of dismissal, the way you brush off an annoying child. No, no, the half-dead ex-inmates insisted, they were quite serious. It was still raining, Abe said. Sliding in the mud, falling down, blackened, scrawny and sick, they beat the Russians that day at soccer. "We felt if we could live through that hell, we could do anything. We could beat them not only because we had all these good plays we knew. No, it was our sense of the miraculous that won that game." Of this story, he gave a well-rehearsed and polished performance the first time the group met.

Once, when asked how he survived, he had said something about a "socialist's prayer" that no one understood and that he did not elaborate upon, despite the perplexity and interest of the group. Risa Eisenstadt, who asked the question, felt she had transgressed, and apologized. Abe's silence established the whole subject as an inviolable domain. Then, during one of the silences that punctuated our last gathering, he began talking.

> You ask how did I survive. I'll tell you. Every morning, I was floating, not here and not there, I was in danger, I told myself, "Abe, you have two tasks. To live another day. To tell the story." That's all. Each morning, I only wanted to sleep, to give in and sleep forever. So I gave myself this talking to, I made myself take this vow, I said to myself these words, "Avrahm! What are you doing? Time to get up! You have two tasks in front of you. To live one more day! To be there when all this is over to tell their story!" So this is the way . . . renewing my vows . . . to the dead . . . and it's still not finished . . . renewing them . . . this is why . . .

He wanted to say: "why I survived." But it was Brodell Borden who whispered the uncompleted sentence.

NOTES

1. Edmond Jabes, *The Book of Questions II* (Middletown: Wesleyan University Press, 1977): p. 29.

2. Jack Kugelmass and Jonathan Boyarin, *From a Ruined Garden: The Memorial Books of Polish Jewry* (New York: Schocken Books, 1983).

Images from the Occupational Years: The Reminiscences of Retirees and Their Implications for Social Work Practice

Doris Francis

Robert Butler's seminal work describing the life review process has led to important insights into the way older persons come to terms with the meaning of their lives and the events they have experienced (Butler, 1963, 1975). The elderly, according to Butler, reappraise and reevaluate their lives through reminiscence, a naturally occurring psychological process, which permits the survey of revived experience, the reexamination of old, unresolved conflicts, and the reintegration of repressed events. This active process of revision of self is shaped by contemporaneous experience; events from the past are interpreted and reinterpreted in the light of present experience.

Life review and reminiscence, according to Butler, help the elderly to cope with late life losses and accept the life cycle. The inevitable crises of age, such as retirement, the death of a loved one, or an increasing awareness of finitude may initiate this life review process and can simultaneously trigger creativity. This paper argues that for older individuals who elect an artistic mode, late life creative expression may reveal and parallel the essential content and process of the traditionally described life review. Here artistic

---

Doris Francis is Assistant Director of Retirees, Municipal Employees Union, Local 237, Adjunct Professor, Graduate Faculty Anthropology and School of Management and Urban Professions, New School for Social Research and President of the Association for Anthropology and Gerontology. She has recently published the prizewinning *Will You Still Need Me, Will You Still Feed Me, When I'm 84?*

activity elaborates released reminiscences into aesthetic artifacts and offers a relatively unexplored dimension for understanding the psychological processes of adult development.

For the medium as well as the content of this newfound artistry, an older artist may reach back into youth or middle years, to family and work experiences. To interpret and integrate one's life and to pass one's knowledge and skills to successive generations are some of the life-review tasks that can be fulfilled through artistic activity. Creative works in memoirs, art, and music may be valuable outcomes of this natural healing process.

Recognizing the importance and function of life review, Butler's work suggests that reminiscence theory has many implications and uses for practitioners in understanding and working with the elderly client and, with some limitations, should be encouraged by gerontologists. One dimension of reminiscence therapy which merits greater exploration, however, is the often neglected area of the meaning to the retired older person of past employment. Indeed, Butler himself emphasizes that "a summation of one's life work is an important aspect of life review therapy" (Butler & Lewis, 1977, p. 269). Akabas underscores the desirability of including work and work institutions as an integral part of all social work practice (Akabas, 1982, pp. 3,32):

> Although social work is intimately involved with people, their coping patterns and their life span, the profession has given limited attention to the many facets of work . . . A concern about the nature of work activities and the workplace . . . would complement and supplement social work's traditional concern for family life and the social role of the family.

Thus to be effective in helping older persons explore, focus, probe, and organize their thinking about the past, the practitioner should not forget the importance of work to people's lives and should be conscious of encouraging the summation of the work experience itself.

A unique opportunity to examine the life review process, as it relates to past occupational experiences and released creative activity was provided by a recent exhibition entitled The World of

Work.[1] The exhibit displayed over ninety folk art productions made prior to the announcement of the exhibition's theme by 17 retired elderly workers. Included were individual works which: (1) directly depicted past work and/or union experiences; (2) employed occupational materials; and/or (3) continued work-related skills. These folk productions (folk art is here defined as art produced by people who lack formal training), enriched by extensive life history interviews conducted by the author, provide rich data for analyzing the theory of the life review process as expressed through creative activity centering on issues related to work.

The goals of an analysis of the folk art and the autobiographical commentary are to determine if the creative process when focused on occupational history, has adaptive value for the creator; to discover if the Butlerian hypothesis regarding the outcomes of reminiscence apply to late life occupational folk art; and to determine if this kind of activity has anything to offer students of social gerontology and human development. The works of nine of the participating artists have been selected as case studies to examine the ways occupational folk art illuminates the life review process.

DIRECT DEPICTIONS OF WORK EXPERIENCES – NEED FOR SELF-ESTEEM

John Hartter worked for 29 years as a water use inspector and retired, reluctantly, in 1977 at the mandatory retirement age. Describing himself, Hartter states: "I guess I never really retired, mentally, from the job." Hartter's papier mache sculptures and drawings reveal his continual revival of unresolved experiences, a carefully detailed recollection of the job scene, and an effort to use humor to come to terms with the indignities and disappointments of his former occupation. In one sculpture, for example, Hartter depicts an inspector turning on his flashlight to read a watermeter and suddenly confronting an enormous water bug. Another depicts the same inspector on his knees, on newspapers, struggling to read a watermeter wedged behind a commode in a cramped, unclean public restroom. Watermeter readers are also shown in Hartter's sketches fending off cobwebs while crouched in basement crawlspaces or standing knee deep in flooded basements.

Wearing a clean, neat uniform and projecting a presentable appearence were important concerns of this intelligent man who, in his off hours, devised innovative technologies to more accurately gauge water usage. Although highly praised, he laments that such devises were never adopted by his superiors, nor in retirement, has he been called back to prepare occupational manuals for training new employees.

Ironically, the only Hartter sculpture which relates to the bureaucratic hierarchy and its hazards for a creative, innovative municipal employee is one showing the rewards of seniority. Here Hartter displays a heavyset, pipesmoking overall-dressed master plumber supervising a scrawny apprentice who is learning to make pipe fittings. Entitled "The Rewards of Seniority," this sculpture evokes a kind of Norman Rockwell nostalgia, as though there once were a system which rewarded the older master. But on another level, Hartter's humor ironically suggests that those at the top of the system may be somewhat lazy and disinterested, letting the younger person do the work for which he receives no credit. It is a system where those who work hard may not be properly rewarded; and where those at the top are not necessarily responsive to the needs and limitations of their staff, nor always deserving of the top position.

For John Hartter, depicting past occupational events with careful details reveals both the humor and the pleasure of his storytelling and the psychologically adaptive value of his late life creativity. Hartter is constantly making sketches of past unresolved events for future art projects and is thereby reexamining and reevaluating these revived experiences. Folk art making for Hartter is the manifestation of the psychologically adaptational process of reminiscence.

A similar effort to reestablish dignity and preserve positive self-image despite a sometimes distasteful job, and also to justify one's life and work, is found in Ike Waksenbaum's pestcontrol sculptures. Dressed in a cutdown version of his former uniform, Waksenbaum's pestcontrol operator looks like a miniaturized adult who holds a metal canister of insecticide. Waksenbaum describes his sculpture of an exterminator as follows.

> The Pest Control operator is POWER. He can do a lot of things . . . He can go into an apartment, he can get the Master Keys to everyplace he wants to go. You have to be loyal, trusty too. And they need you . . . It's one of the headaches at the Housing Authority, the pest. The tenant comes to the manager and he cries. The superintendent calls you in and he says, "Please help me, do something!" They respect this department very much. For me, this exterminator is a Hero. He really does a hell-of-a-good job. Pests are an emergency.
>
> This is like a statue of my twelve years I was with this department and I'm proud.

Dealing with the difficult task of artistically depicting the concept of "pest control" and the irony of making art from killing vermin, Waksenbaum, in a second sculpture, enlarged a paper mache waterbug and then placed a miniaturized man on his back. The rider attempts to control the creature by reining the bug's antennae. This miniaturization of the operator in both sculptures helps Waksenbaum to achieve a sense of psychological control over his past (Dewhurst, 1984).

Like Hartter, the humorous ironic sculptures of Waksenbaum also reveal how retired workers in socially stigmatized jobs or in occupations with unpleasant aspects strive through the life review process to reinterpret ambivalent past experiences so as to maintain positive self-esteem and self-image.[2] For other artists, their work scene representations focus on an earlier, more desireable time period.

Another folk artist, Jacob Lasher, retired due to disability after 38 years as cutter in the textile industry, now sews brightly colored "paintings" which depict his beloved cutting and sewing rooms in a textile factory.

> You can't just stop what you were doing for 38 years and quit cold . . . I did like working in the factory because I was never set up for office work. I tried office work, but I could not take it. I had to be more active and see something that I'd done and accomplish something. I was a cutter. I would see the garment go through and I had that feeling [of accomplishment].

Mr. Lasher's depictions are almost mythologized, generalized remembrances of a job he was forced to leave because of disability and a changing industry.

> The Union's wonderful as far as I was concerned. But then things started happening. Little by little the line fell out, and imports, and going into automation took a lot of the work away. And then we had to make in seven months what another person made in a year. Things started falling off and it wasn't good . . . Imports ruined us. Took a big bite out of the industry.

Lasher's pictures are memory paintings of a time when both he and the textile industry were strong and healthy, and thus these positive images of his past help him deal with late life losses. Interestingly, there are no human figures in his cutting room scene—it remains an image of work tables, the cutting machine, and bolts of cloth, but is empty of human workers. Lasher has created a textile world romanticized for all time, with no mortals who can become disabled, die, or be laid off.

DEPICTING INTERRELATED WORK AND FAMILY EXPERIENCES— NEED FOR INTERGENERATIONAL CONTINUITY

Images from work also inform the artistic productions of folk artists who moved from their place of birth to a new environment, and were thus forced to deal with loss of familiar landscape, kin, and acquaintances. Interestingly, for these relocated artists, their choice of images in late life deal with work scenes remembered from childhood. Vincenzo Ancoma's woven wire sculptures, for example, depict detailed scenes of vineyards and harvests from his native Italy. Clara Johnson's memory paintings show her family and neighbors working on the farm where she grew up in South Carolina.

Another Johnson painting shows the family and children in the kitchen of the Brownsville apartment where they lived for 14 years after moving to New York. This domestic scene of women's work reveals her pride in the fulfillment of her adult role as mother of her own family. Intergenerational continuity is shown by the presence of both her elderly mother and her own young children.

In a third painting, Johnson paints herself in her occupational role as a hospital reception clerk. She describes this job: "I worked in the hospital for 17 years . . . I was a desk clerk, the first person when you walk in, throwing the questions and everything at your face. That was me."

All of Johnson's 17 years of experiences in the hospital are telescoped into this one painting. She places herself in the center at the reception desk with all of the hospital equipment around her in the halls: stretchers, carts, oxygen tanks, wheelchairs; the individual rooms on the floor, with their patients lying in beds, stretch out behind.

The sequence of Johnson's paintings review her past experiences: her life as a young girl in the South, her move to the North as a young mother, and her occupational career later in life when her husband became ill. These pictures form a visual life review revealing her effort to develop a sense of continuity of self through the storytelling details of her paintings. Her creations are also meant to instruct her grandchildren about her past and convey to them significant experiences of her life. Thus her biography is also legitimated and transmitted through her visual depiction of her reminiscences, which are viewed, enjoyed, and cherished by her family and fellow senior center members (Breytspraak, 1984, 110). Here Mrs. Johnson also assumes the traditional role of the elder as the preserver of memories and traditions and as the "teacher of the lessons of experience" to future generations (Coleman, 1974, 1984).

In a similar vein, David Fried's place as a father maintaining the continuity of both his family and their cultural tradition is expressed visually in his hand-carved walking sticks. Fried is a retired navy chaplin with an extensive knowledge of Jewish theology. At birthdays, anniversaries and other life-cycle events he presents hand-carved canes, incised with both Hebrew and English wishes and prayers, to family members. Commemorative coins from his service years in New Guinea, political stickers, and other autobiographical and familiar symbols decorate the canes and give an additional dimension of meaning. Given Fried's wide knowledge of

Biblical lore, these canes can be likened to the staff of a religious leader. And given his role as a *pater familias*, his canes or walking sticks also symbolize guidance, leadership and parental wisdom.

In Fried's scenes, the interrelation of work and family is stressed. And as suggested by the paintings of Johnson discussed above, these dual concerns provide important interrelated areas for the life review process. As Rosabeth Moss Kanter reminds us, the notion of "separate worlds" is a myth: work and the rest of life are inseparable (Kanter, 1977, pp. 7-8).

> The specific intersections and transactions between work and family, between occupations and families are connected organizers of experience and systems of social relations are virtually ignored . . . and are treated separately by many theorists.

CONTINUITY OF TECHNIQUE AND MEDIUM FROM FORMER OCCUPATIONS – NEED FOR SELF-CONSISTENCY

For these artists in the "World of Work" Exhibition whose folk art reveals a connection through medium and technique to their former occupations, their art deals with efforts to cope with their present social position as retired workers, rather than with the ambiguous nature of work life.

Carlo Bergomi uses the same techniques he employed as a master pastry-chef to create rose-decorated ceramic wedding cakes, grape-enclustered vases, and ceramic baskets like those he made from caramelized sugar. "This I worked on like it was a piece of dough; I did it the same way as I used a piece of dough."

Bergomi has achieved much recognition in his senior center because of these unique creations. His trade skills as a master pastry chef cum ceramicist clearly impress center members and staff. By continuing the same work techniques which connect him both physically and psychologically to his past, Bergomi has achieved the pride and continued sense of self he enjoyed as an employed baker.[3] In our consumer society where older people who do not contribute productively are often looked down upon, Bergomi, now in his 80s has maintained self and group esteem by continuing the creative skills which connect him to his productive past.

A similar psychological problem, that of coping with the loss of status at retirement, has been dealt with by Isidore Tolep through his drawings of trees. Tolep, who retired as the manager of a large knitting mill, describes himself as the "head-man," the person to whom all the employees used to turn. He also excelled as a colorist and designer of children's sweaters. "I was one of the best there was in coloring, in coloring sweaters for children." Yet when queried about the possible continuities in technique and skills between his art and his 35 years working in the knitting mill, Tolep snapped, "Forget about my work. That's over." Nonetheless, an examination of his art reveals that his drawing line simulates that of a knitted stitch; and his color areas replicate those of the stripes on the children's sweaters he once designed.

Tolep now concentrates on drawing trees, and admits to achieving a feeling of mastery. Proudly discussing his excellence in the coloration of trees, Tolep echoes Joyce Kilmer: "I think my trees are as good as anybody can make a tree . . . Trees is not hard to make. It's the coloring that makes up the trees."

On a second interview, when greater trust had been established, Tolep confessed to deep feelings of loss on retirement: a loss of position, of work associates, and of social and occupational status. Soon after retirement, his wife died. But now having achieved public recognition of his art work, Tolep has regained a sense of self and group worth comparable to the one he lost on retirement. "When I ran my mill, I was the head man. I was somebody . . . Now, people tell me my trees are as good as anybody can make a tree." It took Tolep ten years to reconstruct this sense of self.

Thus the process of achieving social validation and continuity of self-image after loss of work roles at retirement has been achieved by both Tolep and Bergomi through continued use of work-related skills. The process of art making—the creation of ceramic cakes or the drawing of hundreds of pictures of trees—has enabled both men to adjust to late life losses. For both these artists, the continuity of work skills has contributed positively to achieving continuity of self-concept, despite social loss (Marshall, 1980).

For older folk artists, as for all artists, it is not only achievement in one's own work, but public recognition which enables the individual to build self-regard. Like the process of reminiscence and life review, which Butler suggests are often facilitated by the guidance of an empathic listener who functions as a witness legitimating the meaning of the life story being retold and recreated, so the older person receives necessary validation in public exhibitions where his/her art can be viewed and acknowledged. In the words of Barbara Myerhoff:

> Folk art is a means not only of communication across generations but at the same time assisting the elderly to gain autonomy over their own images. By arranging for elders to present their own artistic works and interpretations of their culture in a context in which they see themselves as major figures, their self-worth and political empowerment are enhanced.
>
> [Exhibitions of older people's folk art] can serve as a model for utilizing the resources of the elderly, heightening our general awareness of them as contributors to the life of a community, and calling attention to the riches they provide in their role as repositories of history and vanished cultures. We must create such occasions, when young and old are brought together, to face each other in the giving and receiving of lives and lore. (1984, p. 38)[4]

This need for social acknowledgement and legitimization is manifested by other artists in the World of Work Exhibition.

Louis Bernstein, a retired printer who lives alone in a windowless basement apartment, arranged for his own public recognition through ingenious means. Bernstein continues his life-long love of paper and printing by constructing sculptures from scraps of paper: the tinfoil from cigarette packs, cream cheese wrappers and the Styrofoam trays from home-delivered meals-on-wheels, are typical materials. Feeling a lack of public standing and recognition, Bernstein linked himself to personages of transcendent power, authority and historical significance by creating silver and gold replicas of the crowns worn by Queen Elizabeth, the Pope, Haile Selassie, the Russian Czar, and other famous people.

> Since I came here, I was all alone. If I didn't do that, I couldn't stay here eight and a half years because this kept me busy. Sometimes I would start maybe 6, 7 in the evening, you know, after I had supper. So I'd stop and look, "Oh my God, it's 7:00 in the morning!" I didn't even know the night passed by because when I did it, I put everything in me. Everything in me to make my art work to be a perfection. If it's not perfection I don't want to do it.

Also, extending the traditional use of paper for writing and correspondence, Bernstein executes small, three-dimensional sculptures which he mails to President Reagan, Princess Margaret, and other luminaries on occasions of birthdays or in cases of accident or illness. Bernstein notes: "When the Queen sees my art work, does she know it comes from a tray of chicken, that it comes from an egg carton?" In exchange for these paper sculptures, Bernstein's mailbox is filled with calligraphied thank-you notes, written on embossed stationery, and sealed with elegant stamps. "Dear Mr. Bernstein: I am commanded by the Queen to thank you for your beautiful handmade card." Bernstein has thus achieved through his paper sculptures his own social recognition and the reflected appraisals of a special audience.

SUMMARY AND CONCLUSIONS

Butler's work has suggested that reminiscence is an active, interpretative, constructive and appropriate activity for the elderly, and that the life review has many implications and uses for practitioners in understanding and working with the older client. This paper has stressed the adaptive functions of reminiscence for nondepressed subjects and has paid special attention to the way the creation of folk art expresses the life review process, making manifest the reexamination of unresolved conflicts and the need for self-consistency and self-validation that are not always articulated verbally. This research also confirms Lewis' finding that those who reminisced experienced an increase in the consistency of their past and present self-concepts (Lewis, 1971).

Much exciting work has appeared in numerous disciplines building on Butler's writing about the importance and function of life review in understanding the psychological processes of the elderly. Myerhoff, the anthropologist, for example, utilizes Butler's findings to reveal how "the old point the way to the search through life experience from the perspective of the present, sorting and rearranging the past for the understanding that is required before it is too late." Memory, she adds,

> . . . is a continuum, ranging from vague, dim shadows to the brightest, most vivid totality of an original experience. It may offer opportunity not merely to recall the past but to relive it, in all its primary freshness, unaltered by intervening changes and reflections. Such magical Proustian moments are pinpoints of the greatest intensity, when a sense of the past as never truly lost is experienced. The diffuseness of life is then transcended, the sense of duration overcome, and all of one's self and one's memories are felt to be universally valid. Simultaneity replaces sequence and a sense of oneness with one's past is achieved. Often such moments involve childhood memories, and then one experiences the self as it was originally, and knows beyond doubt that one is still the same person as the child who yet dwells within a time-altered body. Integration through memory with earlier states of being surely provides the sense of continuity and completeness that may be counted as an essential developmental task of old age. (1984, p. 319)

However, despite the rich heritage from Butler's research, much of the literature on the life review process has centered on the importance of childhood memories, earlier states, and family history, rather than paying attention to the entire life cycle and "the tying of the life cycle and institutions into a meaningful whole" (Erikson, 1977, p. 112). Through analysis of the occupational folk art creations of retirees, this paper has demonstrated that experiences from the middle years of employment also provide rich material for the reflectiveness and newly released creativity of the later years. This finding should be considered in any complete analysis of reminiscence and the psychological processes of adult development and incorporated into intervention strategies. Through active efforts and "enriching" interventions, the practitioner can provide encouragement and the necessary social conditions and contexts for older persons to use images from their past lives to actively work toward self-development, a sense of wholeness, and a coherent view of the life cycle.[5]

NOTES

1. The World of Work: An exhibition of Occupational Folk Art by Retirees, cosponsored by the Municipal Employees Union, Local 237 I.B.T. and The Elder Craftsmen, Inc., co-curated by Doris Francis and Geri Wasserman. The World of Work was exhibited at the NCOA Gallery Patina, Washington, DC, the Local 237 Gallery, and the Robert F. Wagner Labor Archives, New York University.

2. The writings of Sennett and Cobb, Terkel and Blauner extend this discussion to issues confronting the worker throughout his/her work life. (Sennett & Cobb, 1973; Terkel, 1974; Blauner, 1967.) The recent analysis of Kaufman explores the processes of reinterpretation of self (Kaufman, 1986).

3. Marshall makes the interesting suggestion that this process of reminiscence may help older persons maintain a sense of esteem by allowing them to identify their present situation with a highly valued past and thus make status claims based on the past (Marshall, 1980, p. 108.)

4. The work of Kahana and Coe (1969) suggests how significant it is for practioners to encourage older persons to retain important images from the past in situations which have the potential to depersonalize them by stripping them of their past (Breytspraak, 1984, p. 127.)

5. "If we were interested in how people go about interpreting and making sense of themselves as they age, we must *start* with their interpretations, not with an investigator's attempt to preconceive . . . the dimensions assumed to be relevant . . . We may need to start with methods from which we can derive older people's interpretations of themselves—for example, through autobiographies, life-history, untutored artistic productions, and conversations in which we can observe at first hand the negotiation of meanings, the making of attributions, and the rearranging of goals actually in progress" (Breytsraak, 1984, pp. 121-122).

REFERENCES

Akabas, S. H. Work: the vital connection. *Practice*, 1982, 5(2), 3, 32-34.

Blauner, R. *Alienation and freedom: the factory worker and his industry*. Chicago: University of Chicago Press, 1967.

Breytspaak, L.M. *The development of self in later life*. Boston: Little, Brown & Company, 1984.

Butler, R. The life review: an interpretation of reminiscence in the aged. *Psychiatry*, 1975, 893-900.

Butler, R. and Lewis, M.I. *Aging and mental health*. St. Louis: C. V. Mosby, 1977.

Coleman, P. G. Measuring reminiscence characteristics from conversation as adaptive features of old age. *International Journal of Aging and Human Development*, 1974, 5(3), 281-294.

Coleman, P. G. The value of reminiscence in adaptation to old age. Longitudinal care studies over ten years. In D. B. Bromley (Ed.), *Gerontology: Social and behavioural perspectives*. London: Croom Helm, 1984.

Dewhurst, C.K. The arts of working: manipulating the urban work environment. *Western Folklore*, 1984, 43(3), 192-202.

Erikson, E. *Toys and reasons: stages in the ritualization of experience*. New York: Norton, 1977.

Havighurst, R. J. and Glasser, R. An exploratory study of reminiscence. *Journal of Gerontology*, 1972, 27, 235-253.

Kahana, E. and Coe, R. M. Self and staff conceptions of institutionalized aged. *The Gerontologist*, 1969, 9, 264-267.

Kaminsky, M. Pictures from the past: the use of reminiscence in casework with the elderly. *Journal of Gerontological Social Work*, 1978, 1(1), 19-32.

Kanter, R. M. *Work and the family in the United States: a critical review and agenda for research and policy*. New York: Russel Sage Foundation, 1977.

Kastenbaum, R. Time course and time perspective in later life. In C. Eisdorfer (Ed.), *Annual Review of Gerontology and Geriatrics*, 1982, III, New York: Springer.

Kurzman, P. A. and Akabas, S. H. Industrial social work as an arena for practice. *Social Work*, 1981, 52-59.

Lewis, C. N. Reminiscing and self-concept in old age. *Journal of Gerontology*, 1971, 26, 240-243.

Marshall, V. W. *Last chapters: a sociology of aging and dying*. Monterey, CA: Brooks/Cole, 1980.

McMahon, A. and Rhudick, P. H. Reminiscing's adaption significance in the aged. *Archives of General Psychiatry*, 1964, 10, 292-298.

Merriam, S. The concept and function of reminiscence: a review of the research. *The Gerontologist*, 1980, 20, 604-609.

Myerhoff, B. Rites and signs of ripening: the intertwining of ritual, time, and growing older. In D. I. Kertzer and J. Keith (Eds.), *Age and anthropological theory*. Ithaca: Cornell University Press, 1984.

Myerhoff, B. Life not death in Venice: the transmission of an endangered tradition. *Festival of American Folklife Program Book*, Washington, DC: Smithsonian Institution, 1984, 36-38.

Pincus, A. Reminiscence in aging and its implications for social work practice. *Social Work*, 1970, 156, 47-53.

Sciorra, J. *Crafts*. Unpublished paper, n.d.

Sennett, R. and Cobb, J., *The hidden injuries of class*. New York: Knopf, 1973.

Terkel, S. *Working*. New York: Pantheon, 1974.

The Young, the Old, and the Life Review: Report on a Brookdale Project

Robert Disch

In May 1984, the Brookdale Center on Aging received a grant from the John A. Hartford Foundation to design and operate a demonstration project in intergenerational life-history work utilizing teenagers and frail elderly from New York City. The funding was scheduled to run for two and one-half years with the option for a no-cost extension if required. When the project ended in September, 1987, approximately 103 teenagers had interviewed 447 elderly people in a wide variety of gerontological institutions and private homes.

MAJOR GOALS AND OBJECTIVES

The project was designed to generate outcomes that resulted from the *process* of conducting life-history interviews and other, *tangible* outcomes designed to extend the life of the project beyond the funding period. The "process" objectives were to:

- Give the target population – isolated and frail elderly – the opportunity to reminiscence, to tell their life stories.
- Meet the needs of isolated elderly for social contact with young people; enable them to overcome feelings of loneliness, loss of connection, and depression brought on by illness and

Robert Disch is Director of the Hartford Intergenerational Life History Project of the Brookdale Center on Aging and Managing Editor of the *Values, Ethics and Aging: The Journal of Human Values and Aging*.

isolation; broaden their communication with the outside world.

—Help prepare the young for school and work by building crucial skills: writing, interviewing, coping with deadlines, organizing information, editing tapes, carrying tasks to completion, accepting responsibility, enhancing interpersonal skills, hearing and utilizing constructive criticism.

—Provide young people with role models and mentors—the homebound and frail elderly whose life histories would give them living examples of responsibility, maturity, and endurance, as well as the historical perspective that is necessary to move beyond the perpetual now of the culture of youth; and help them learn to participate responsibly in the political processes of the larger world.

—Foster the transmission of ethnic heritage and cultural legacies through enabling the young and the old to work together on life history projects.

—Provide young and old with the opportunity to acquire more positive attitudes about each other through mutual interaction and partnership in a common project.

—Give each elderly participant copies of the anthology that contains his/her work and a tape of the interview for personal use or to pass on to future generations.

—Help the elderly use the life review process to resolve conflict and integrate unassimilated life experience; help them see their lives as a whole in the context of the historical period in which they lived.

The project was also designed to generate tangible outcomes that could be used to replicate this project, create similar projects and stimulate thinking about the uses of reminiscence as a tool for working with the elderly. These included:

—*Life History Video Tape*.* In collaboration with the Brooklyn College Television Center Brookdale produced a video tape on intergenerational life review work.

---

*Denotes material available from the Brookdale Center on Aging of Hunter College, 25 East 25th Street, New York, NY 10010.

—*Life Stories Manual.** A crucial part of this Project was the creation of a *Manual on Life Stories* that would be "state of the art." To the best of our knowledge, such a booklet did not exist. Materials for the completed book were gathered from extensive field work, research and weekly meetings with a group of interested social workers and life review experts who met between September 1986 and August 1987.

—*The Journal of Gerontological Social Work.** This publication was one of the tangible outcomes of the project.

—*Anthologies.** Throughout the course of the Project we produced anthologies that contained representative selections from the interviews.

—*Evaluation.** After a year and a half, we completed a formal evaluation of the project.

MAJOR OUTCOMES

The following pages will provide a brief report on this project, highlighting those areas that were most relevant to achieving the stated objectives and which are likely to be of interest to others working in the field of intergenerational life review.

Selection of Cooperating Institutions

Throughout the course of the project it became increasingly obvious to us that the choice of collaborating institutions to a large extent determined the degree of success or failure of that particular segment of the program. The selection was not, of course, the only reason for success or failure, but in some cases selecting the wrong institution did result in a waste of time and money. We learned that not all geriatric institutions, no matter how elevated their reputations, necessarily make good settings for intergenerational life-history work, at least work of the quality we aimed for. As we gained experience we realized that our project worked best when participating staff wanted the project to work for the benefit of their populations. In institutions where the project was, for whatever reasons, viewed as an irritant or source of extra work for the staff, the impact was severely diminished if not quite eliminated altogether.

In larger geriatric institutions we found that it was necessary to involve several (often baronial) departments—social services, recreation, volunteers, food service (for socials)—to obtain the best results. In short, the project ran smoothly where the director as well as the department heads and their assistants understood the importance of the project, agreed with the goals and methods, and actively wanted to make it succeed.

If all of these pieces aren't in place, little works or works only in aggravating fits and starts. One week the elderly are ready for the interviews. The next week the students arrive to find everyone off on a visit to the Methodist Church or out on a picnic. Often appointments are made for clients by one department without consultation with those responsible for the life history work.

The essential point is that all the participants must be truly cooperative. They must be willing to help explain the project to their clientele, make lists of volunteers, provide storage for tape recorders, help arrange appointments, find relatively quiet spaces for interviews and cheerfully assist in the solution of unanticipated problems. They should also be prepared to monitor the elderly participants to ensure that the process is not having any undesirable side-effects. If such cooperation cannot be readily obtained, the solution is to go elsewhere, if such is possible. A more admirable but arduous route is to try to instill in the key people the enthusiasm that should be there from the start. The worst scenario is to attempt to do a project where the staff is indifferent or overtly hostile.

Recruiting Older Adult Participants

When the director and key staff people are knowledgeable about and in support of the project, it is not difficult to find willing participants in geriatric institutions. Things are more complicated with frail elderly who remain at home. In live-in facilities, staff intuitively know who to approach for interviewing and who to pass over. Making these and similar decisions is part of the daily routine. Many homebound, on the other hand, may not have even monthly interaction with a social worker or other professional who is reasonably familiar with the client's mental/emotional condition. It is also difficult to monitor the interview process and the latent reactions, if any.

In order to protect the integrity of the entire process and to guard against undesirable outcomes, the project director established a policy that all participants—in or out of institutions—be referred by a geriatric professional working with the interviewee or a family member who was in frequent contact. We also insisted on a post-interview procedure (phone calls or visits) by the referral person to make sure that no negative events were provoked by the interview.

These somewhat elaborate safeguards are the result of Butler's (1963, pp. 271-73) warning that "Constructive outcomes to the life review are not invariable . . . severe depression, states of panic, intense guilt, and constant obsessional ruminations" might follow from the reminiscence process. Since this project was not intended to be "therapeutic" in the clinical sense, we elected to work with mentally and emotionally stable people who could willingly volunteer for interviewing.

By following these procedures, we recruited only people who were functioning within fairly "normal" boundaries. Throughout the course of the interviews, the students were encouraged to let the instructor know about any problems they were encountering or any untoward or aberrant behaviors they might be noticing. (All students, of course, were instructed as to procedures to follow if a homebound client took ill, started crying, refused to continue with the interview or indicated some other problem.)

By insisting on a careful screening of participants (including the teenagers), monitoring the progress of the interviews, training the students in the appropriate ways of terminating visits, and utilizing post-interview follow-ups (by phone and direct visits), we managed to avoid a single negative outcome in hundreds of interviews. If there was one, we did not learn of it. Certainly no subject "went to pieces"—a fear often voiced about reminiscence work.

The reasons for this go beyond the fact that our interviewees were both selected and self-selecting. Clinically depressed people were not invited to participate, nor did any who knew of the project volunteer. But such an exclusion was—on our part at least—hardly necessary. In most instances, people who are not suited for interlocutor-present life review involvement are capable of finding ways to avoid it.

Even perfectly "normal" people appear to have the capacity to maintain adequate distance from material that threatens or disturbs. According to a Brookdale colleague, Arthur Strimling, a much-practiced life review expert,

> There seems to be a natural restraint built into these relationships that keeps them within emotionally manageable bounds. Not that we don't hear tales of incredible suffering, loss, betrayal, survival and triumph. We do, constantly, but no one is required to tell anything they don't want to tell, and again, most of us find that the old are much more emotionally resilient than we first think . . .

Recruiting and Working with the Young

In the beginning of this project, we elected to work with four groups of teenagers from widely different social, ethnic and institutional backgrounds. These included teenagers from a Lutheran Church group, students from a Summer Youth Corps program, members of the N.Y. City Volunteer Corps and juniors and seniors from the Hunter College High School. With the exception of the CVC Corps, all student participants were at least titular volunteers. The CVC members, on the other hand, were assigned to do Life History work as part of their weekly duties.

Three of the four groups received some type of salary or stipend for participating in the project. Yet, there was no significant difference in the dropout rate between the paid and unpaid cohorts (dropout rates averaged between 8 and 12% for all groups). Nor did the prospect of receiving pay appear to influence recruiting in any significant way. The conclusions that might cautiously be drawn from our experience are that some teenagers find that they do not want to do this kind of work (no matter how carefully the project is explained to them beforehand) and second, the dropout rate is likely to be the same for those who are paid to do it as for those who are unpaid. In all, the unpaid volunteers from the Lutheran Church group had the lowest dropout rate. This undoubtedly can be explained by the fact that teens who voluntarily affiliate with church groups are likely to be more serious (perhaps more mature) than, say, kids in a summer youth program.

Based on our experience we recommend that no student be assigned to do life history work if the student objects; that no form of punishment follow if a student wishes to drop out after the program begins; and that no student ever be rigorously discouraged from dropping out if he/she seriously wishes to do so. Yet, this advice should not be construed to rule out encouraging timid, introverted or reticent students to participate or to try again if they wash out on the first couple of interviews. Often these are the very students who will most benefit if they can find the ways to solve the problems that are discouraging them. How these matters are dealt with is the responsibility of the adults who supervise and instruct the teenagers.

In general, we found that the busier the students were in other aspects of their lives, the more important it was that the project be well organized and efficiently run. When such did not occur because of adult failure to produce, the teens quickly became disaffected and demoralized. This is all the more reason why participating institutions must be fully involved with the project and why administrators must keep all of the commitments they make in the beginning of the project.

Of all these commitments, the most important is unquestionably that of helping the individual teenagers become members of a functioning life history support group. As the group evolves, the students should feel free to discuss their feelings and emotions as well as practical matters regarding their deepening involvement with the frail elderly. Like selection of the right cooperating institutions, the development of a coherent, supportive group will go a long way toward reaching all of the goals of the project.

The Magic: Young Meet Old

What happens to the young and old who meet in this kind of project? While formal evaluation is difficult, most attempts report beneficial outcomes for both young and old. Still, much of our best information comes from participant reports, audio tapes of interviews, staff observations, anecdotes and other "subjective" sources that should not be underestimated by evaluators.

Certainly the teenagers appear to become less stereotyped in their thinking about the aged and some elderly tell us that they "didn't realize there were so many good kids out there." Since both age cohorts draw much of their view of the world from the distortions of the mass media, what else should we expect?

Beyond modified stereotyping, deeper, more significant changes occur. In a recent issue of the Brookdale Newsletter, the author speculated that life history work can expedite the process of social maturation in the adolescent (Brookdale Newsletter, Winter 1986, P. 1 and ff.). Our observations throughout the course of the project strongly suggest that successful involvement in a life history project involves the teenagers in experiences antithetical to the "presentism" and the self-obsession so characteristic of adolescence, that the work compensated for lost or diminished routes to social and emotional maturity.

Another outcome of a well-run project for the students is the sheer opportunity to learn about human existence and history in the form of personal witness. On one tape we encounter the following story told by an 84-year-old Jewish man whose life sounds much like that of the hero of Abraham Cahan's story *Yekl: A Tale of the New York Ghetto* (better known as the film *Hester Street*). At age 5 "Manny" arrived in America, four and a half years after his father. His story takes one into the imaginative worlds of Michael Gold in *Jews Without Money*, Henry Roth, in *Call it Sleep* and other stories of little kids hustling around the intense, dangerous streets of the lower East Side without the protective intercession of strong, supportive fathers. A natural athlete, Manny survived by insinuating his way onto the athletic teams of St. Mary's Church. There he found a coach who "played fair," putting two Jewish kids on the Irish team because they were the best for the positions. Here's an excerpt from his interview:

> Then there was a St. Mary's church there, there was a fellow, Bob, a recreation teacher, and he started basketball teams, I remember. Cause I was very athletic as a kid, it just happens. That was already a year or two later. See, I learned how to speak English and we got along pretty good and I got onto the team with the Irish. There was only two Jewish kids on there and we used to meet in the church and Bob used to be our

coach and we used to challenge different places. When we went to the Police Athletic League we challenged a team representing them. But, this Bob was very fair. Like if I tried out for right field . . . and somebody else tried out for right field—one fellow thought he had pull—you know how kids are. But Bob would say, sit down, he's better for the position. So there used to be animosity there, but still they were sports about it. Bob said it, that was the end of it. So public school 12 closed up when I was in about the sixth grade and I went to rapid advanced class, they used to call it. I went to public school 147 on Henry Street. Then I was already known as Blackie and I was already on the basketball team there, and I was on the baseball team. See I personally had it very good because I was an athlete, but I was also very good in school. . . . I got a job after school working at the Odeon Theater on Clinton Street to sell candies, apples, whatever they gave me to sell, and I used to work on like commission. So I was always ambitious to have a basketball. So I finally saved up two dollars and I bought a basketball. My father came and said only bums play ball and he took the basketball and he cut it up. I was working three weeks to get that basketball. That, I never forgot that incident. I thought that was the meanest guy in the world. I never had any use for him after that. We were never any close to start with cause I didn't know him for the first five years, but as far as I knew him I know he used to come in the saloon, he used to come in drunk half the time, when he cut that basketball up, all my life I, I just, not that I didn't forgive him, but I just had no use for him. I figured he was a man without feeling, you know. And that's what I . . . my mother . . . we got along very well, you see, and my father was estranged with me all the years, never really sat down and talked to me, you know, as a son and father, cause he was always busy with his cronies, but that there basketball . . . this I'll never forget. In other words, he didn't understand . . . at the same time he must have loved me very much, too, because when I went after school sometimes to the yeshiva, you know, on Henry Street, and one time I asked a question to a rabbi, "What is God?" you know, a little kid. So the rabbi took a big ruler, he hit me such a whack my hand swelled up like that.

> Instead of answering the question, he hit me on the hand. When my father saw that he ran to school, he was going to kill the teacher, I'm telling you. The teacher ran away, he didn't show up there for a month. But it was, you know, a stupid way of teaching that time. The rabbi was . . . my mother used to say, "The rabbi hit you, you must have deserved it." I said, all I asked was a question, I said what is God, who is He, I can't see Him. I mean it was a question. But that was the answer I got. So he must have loved me because it hurt him very much. I realized later on how much it hurt him when he saw my hand swell up like that. So I'd say that the upbringing they had was awfully ignorant. They didn't understand their children, they didn't understand themselves. They had a tough life to start with, they used to work, you know, very hard on a truck, carry those bags of flours. Then when I used to come home he had no time for children. So he used to go out for a drink with other truckers and then come in. After a while they'd go to the saloon. So children were like an outside thing to them. Only they probably loved their children in their own way, but they just didn't understand it, they didn't understand the needs, you know. Like I was very good in school, I went to high school, then I had to drop out, you know, couldn't finish because there was no money and there was no encouragement there, you know, not because they didn't want us but . . . so I started to learn a trade at the time, you know what I mean? So instead of following up my athletics and things like that I was already busy trying to help support the house, bring in a few dollars here, a few dollars there. And that was the childhood.

When a student encounters a storyteller of Manny's stature a lot of valuable things happen beyond the immediate benefit for the participants.

First, the group gets an opportunity to hear an incredibly interesting story about a little kid who survived the Lower East Side by besting the tough Irish boys at their own games. The tape provides fascinating first-person social history with significance for understanding both the immigrant experience and the process of assimilation. Few surviving narratives reveal with such clarity the distaste for American athletics that was prevalent among Jewish immigrants around the turn of the century. The sliced up basketball, for instance, is one of those classic stories that are the dream of the social historian and of great value to classroom teachers.

And beyond the social history is the psychological story, that of Manny's unresolved conflict with his father, that the interview so poignantly reveals.

In this story some of the Butlerian claims for the reminiscence process appear close to fulfillment. All participants including the instructor learn a valuable psychological lesson about the resolution of conflicting feelings about people close—or not close enough—to Manny and, perhaps, to us all. Some adolescents are ready to hear the message, others are not now but may recall this type of psychosocial survival story years later.

For Manny, there was an obvious joy and empowerment in the act of participating in the interview. His eagerness for and gusto in the telling was obvious to anyone involved in the event. Of great importance, for him, was the dialogue about his father: "I never had any use for him . . . "; "I was estranged with him all my life . . . " (sic); "He must of been a man of no feelings"; "Yet, he'd must have loved me very much . . . "; "They had no time for kids. . . . " Here is a well adjusted man (he had been happily remarried at 80 and was very content with life in general) struggling to resolve conflict and find a way to forgive.

At this point we reach the limits of life history work as it was practiced in this project. A therapist would undoubtedly have followed up on the story about the father and other tempting leads. The student did not and it's probably better that way. The uninitiated should not attempt therapy in life history work. But we can at least go away strongly suspecting that Manny knows something about his father that he didn't quite "get" before. If the outcomes turn out to be "therapeutic," so much the better.

REFERENCE

Robert Butler, "The Life Review: An Interpretation of Reminiscence in the Aged," *Psychiatry* 26 (1963): 65-76.

Transformation: Life Review and Communal Theater

Susan Perlstein

With the greying of America, a revival of interest in storytelling traditions has emerged. This reawakened awareness of a more personalized way of passing on history, culture and tradition has taken on a variety of forms. Oral history, a formal framing of one's personal tales within a broader context, sheds new light on how we interpret historical events. Life review, a more personal recounting and reassessing of one's life experience, has become an important therapeutic tool in working with the elderly.

Before beginning on a life review project, it is important to clarify the purpose of the interview because of the many uses that can be made of the life review materials. Often a tape or transcript of the individual narrative is prepared for the personal use of the client and his/her family, friends or caregivers. In group work with the elderly, life review interviews can be shared with peers to celebrate the stories that must be told. Youngsters may conduct interviews in order to learn from the elderly. In the public arena, historians, anthropologists, psychologists, social workers, English teachers and theater people look to life review as part of the discipline of their work. Other uses of life narrative include the enhancing of our understanding of social history. A life review project can also be used to build a sense of community within a given institution or neighborhood. The question of how to transform the information, both fact and feelings, into a usable, coherent form for both the teller and

---

Susan Perlstein is Founder and Director of Elders Share the Arts, which has just celebrated its 8th Anniversary. Her innovative use of the life review with frail elderly can be seen in her recent video production, *Elder Voices*.

the receivers of the stories, is a central concern of the work of Elders Share the Arts, a community arts organization in New York City committed to the goal of improving the scope and quality of creative arts and humanities programs for the elderly. ESTA has cultivated an ethnically and racially diverse staff of professional artists, folklorists and social workers who conduct workshops and training sessions based on the uses of life review and life history.

One important aspect of the ESTA program is the development of living history theater, a dramatic genre in which older adult participants share their life stories and create original plays from the collective accounts. In the group process, members reinterpret the historical and sociocultural framework of their life stories. These stories are transformed into a theater piece and performed as a celebration of community life. The process of creating a living history theater play addresses issues of personal growth, cultural identity and community empowerment. The process of life review is transformed into a theater art form (Perlstein 1981).

In this paper, I will first examine some theoretical aspects of the life review process, then explore an example of the transformation of cultural heritage from one living history theater group, and lastly discuss the uses of these life review materials for other formats.

THEORETICAL CONSIDERATIONS

In approaching life review work in general, one asks how the group's identity was forged, fought for, undermined, resurrected and reclaimed. For example, in selecting life stories for living history plays, a historical context is essential to braid the often broken threads of the past remembrances into a cohesive strand. In the process of creating a living history play, the group members are asked to find these threads and weave them into a tapestry of the group's social and cultural history.

Cultural history is an important survival mechanism for the elderly. Many social scientists who study the problems facing the elderly agree on the significance of culture in coping and adapting to losses. In a critique of the current literature on ethnicity and aging, Carol Holzberg argues that it is the cultural dimensions rather than the social class that can best facilitate adjustment to the constraints of aging. She says:

> Ethnicity based on shared history, collective identity, sense of peoplehood, unique heritage, tradition, common expectations, values, attitude and meaningful symbols is a significant influence upon the process of aging. (Holzberg, p. 256)

To achieve better understanding of the coping mechanisms of the elderly, information is needed on how individual life experiences have been influenced by country of origin, historical point of entry, process of acculturation and social integration. Given the high percentage of elderly who are out of the labor force, pride and self-esteem derived from past cultural history are playing an increasingly significant role in the quality of life of the elderly.

Particular developmental needs of the elderly are addressed through living history theater. From a psychological perspective, the process of life review enables the elder to affirm his/her understanding and experience, share it with a community, and in performance pass on the legacy. Erikson writes that the primary psychosocial task in the last phase of the life cycle is that of coming to terms with one's life, of finding self-acceptance and the psychosocial unity he named "ego integrity" (Erikson, 105). All too often the elderly find themselves isolated, depressed and despairing of their situation. They find little consolation in facing the end of their lives. A topic dealt with in the well known essay on life review by Dr. Robert Butler. He argued that for many people the process of psychic reintegration through reminiscence has the positive value of building self-esteem (1963).

Through living history theater, the elder connects the triumphs and defeats in his/her life to social and historical events with others' past experience. In this life review process, individuals often see themselves as part of a continuum and gain a greater sense of well-being by affirming their connection to a larger community. Barbara Myerhoff writes eloquently on the importance of providing a place to discover and affirm historical continuity.

> Continuity is a fundamental necessity for human life, collectively and individually. It is central to social gatherings of all sorts, when people assemble to experience their interdependence and overcome their human separateness. It is central to culture, the shared life ways of a group, which has continued and persevered over time. Continuity is essential for psychological well-being and personal integration, for an individual to experience him/herself as one person, despite change and disruption throughout the life cycle. Ultimately continuity figures largely at the end of life, when the individual devises ways to fend off the possibility of complete extinction. (Myerhoff, *Life's Career,* p. 164)

Living history theater addresses four kinds of continuities: social, cultural, spiritual and personal.

In addition, social scientists write about the human need for personal history to be linked to shared collective experience. Members of an ethnic group connect to other's lives through shared parentage, family, kinship and history. Shared arts, religions, literature, myths and beliefs also link people.

> These linkages help make tolerable the individual's existence that is otherwise intolerably bounded by its own fragile aloneness, its own birth and death. The element of the shared past, of its own history and origins is deeply embedded in every individual's personal identity: it is part of the basic group identity with which each personal identity is inseparably molded. (Myerhoff, Rites, p. 305)

Cultural anthropologists talk about life review in the context of studying the transmission of traditions through both sacred and secular ritual. For Barbara Myerhoff, an anthropologist who worked extensively with the elderly, understanding ritual was a crucial aspect of her work. Ritual has always been prominent in those areas of life that are characterized by uncertainty, anxiety, impotence and disorder. The process of reinventing ritual helps the elderly to understand the continuity from past to present. Through ritual, new events are connected to preceding ones and incorporated into a stream of precedents so that they are recognized as growing out of tradition and experience. By stating enduring and underlying patterns, ritual connects past, present and future, transcending history and time (Myerhoff, *Rites*, p. 309).

In the form of living history theater, a conscious attempt is made to link the lives of participants to each other and to past history in a performed cultural event. The play addresses the historical, psychological and cultural needs of the elderly by providing a process that Myerhoff calls "a definitional ceremony." In *Number Our Days* she describes such a ceremony as an enacted social drama that repeats itself for an audience. Both the subjects and audience recognize the scene as a cultural mirror which reflects collective knowledge (Myerhoff, p. 32).

In a society that denigrates the elderly, creating forms for enhancing their position is vital to the well-being of that community. According to Myerhoff, cultural situations that promote severe invisibility among the aged call for symbolic and ritual elaborations that promote a way of being, a way of becoming visible. Immigrant populations, for example, sharply and permanently cut off from their native roots, populations that expect ideological or biological extinction, groups that have lost natural progeny who can carry forward traditions, people and collectives that have no natural heirs to validate their individual claims to have lived a worthy life: these are some of the situations that create a need for the elderly to dramatize and ritually display their own version of themselves and their histories. So performance is more than just a way to be seen. According to Myerhoff, "performance gives one self-definition, and that is tantamount to being what one claims to be" (*Telling*, p. 25). In living history theater, the enactments are intentional. They address important social and cultural issues. The plays are an example of definitional ceremony – "They tame the chaos of the world, at once asserting both existence and meaning" (Myerhoff, *Telling*, p. 25).

LIVING HISTORY THEATER

The elderly traditionally embodied the voice of history, wisdom and knowledge learned from past experience. As a group the elderly must cope with issues of integrity and self-acceptance, essential tasks in the last stage of the life cycle. In discussing one example of living history theater groups, one can observe the ways in which the play process helps to integrate past, present and future cultural patterns.

Working Hands, a living history play by the Hodson Senior Center Drama Group provides an example of the collective use of individual life reviews for the transmission of culture for a group of elderly black women. Like other senior centers, the members come to the center for lunch, recreational activities and social services. Since 1976, the drama group participants, aged 65 to 90, have met for weekly workshops in which they share stories, learn theater skills and develop and rehearse plays.

Completed in 1983, *Working Hands* consisted of a collage of scenes depicting work stories of the thirteen black women in the group. In Act I, "Hands at Home," the group depicted housework in the 1920s. Scenes showed taking care of the children, cooking, and cleaning. In Act II, "Hands on the Job," the group enacted work in a factory, in a department store and in a restaurant during the 1940s. The last act, "Hands in the Community," depicted a scene from the House of Jazz, a neighborhood school where volunteers taught children about jazz. In the grand finale, the chorus sang about the activities of each group member at the senior center. The audience joined in a jazzy version of "She's Got the Whole World in Her Hands."

Living history theater plays develop from collected stories on a theme. The collective image for *Working Hands* started with a life review exercise. In a group poem, each member was asked to look at her hands, touch them and visualize them at work. We clapped a rhythm to the words "hand, hands at work," and in between the refrain each person spoke about the activity her hands remembered. Some women spoke about sewing, cooking, cleaning, and caring for their children, relatives and friends. Others spoke of working as domestics, cooks and laborers. Others talked about activities like caring for plants and playing music. The group loved the poem and decided to deepen its understanding of the remembrances. For the next few weeks, we listened to work stories. Members felt drawn to reenacting Bernice's story which became the focus for the central theme of the play. Bernice and her story exemplified how an individual experience can symbolize significant issues for the group. In the process of creating the play, members of the group helped integrate the theme in their present lives.

In the life review poem, Bernice contributed the line "my hands like to play the piano." When later asked to share a story about the piano, she began by saying that although she worked her entire adult life as a secretary, she wished she had become a professional jazz musician. She was an only child of a black sharecropper who moved North to work in construction and married an immigrant Jamaican who worked as a domestic. Like many other immigrant parents, Bernice's mother hoped her daughter would do better than she had. Though she too loved music, she never had the time to indulge her passion. All of her life she encouraged Bernice to study the piano. On the other hand, her father, a religious churchgoing man, had traditional expectations for Bernice. She should learn to cook, sew, clean house and get married.

As a teenager, Bernice hung out with Dizzie Gillespie and improvised jazz much to her father's dismay. As an adult, she gave up the piano to please her father, but never married. The drama group reenacted a scene of a parental argument from Bernice's childhood. Bernice role-played her mother. In a loud voice she exclaimed: "I want Bernice to play the piano. She should have opportunities I never had." Her father yelled back, "No daughter of mine will play that downright sinful music." Through role play, Bernice was able to see her story more objectively and separate herself from her parents conflict, a resolution she had not been able to work through.

In looking back, the other group members also shared stories of parental conflict over morality, religion, work and urban living in raising a black girl in New York City. Through role play, Bernice and the group came to see role as a process of socialization, role as a cultural pattern, role as a social norm, and role as an assigned performance. The complex interwoven conflicts that encompass class, race and gender expectations revealed themselves in Bernice. She felt caught between jazz and the church, the bad sexy girl and the good family woman, between choosing an autonomous independent pathway different from her mother and the traditional feminine role.

In all these situations, the individual chooses to defy or accept the expected behavior. At seventy, Bernice could decide for herself how she felt about music, religion and sex. The group encouraged Bernice to play the piano. By the culmination of work on the play, Bernice found new energy and excitement in her chosen role as an important, talented musical contributor to the group. In the final scene, set in the community today, another member asked Bernice to accompany her on the piano. Lillian instructed children in a local music school about jazz. Bernice gladly accompanied Lillian, as they taught the audience "Dark Town Strutter's Ball." What a ball for Bernice, the drama group and the audience as they saw unfolding before them a resolution to Bernice's painful childhood dilemma, and a reaffirmation of the unity, courage and vitality by the black women who could now let loose and sing both jazz and gospel. Here the tension between the religious gospel and urban jazz merged to create a cohesive play, held together by the common beat from the black church to the city-run center.

And so, the musical form derived from gospel both symbolized and realized the survival of black culture. The definitional ceremony for Bernice, the group and the audience came in recognition of the continuity and unity of their cultural heritage from gospel to jazz. The powerful and painful conflicts that immobilized Bernice in her particular life, and which others identified with, helped the community of elderly who witnessed the play to join in a celebration of acceptance for the contradictions within themselves, the group and the community. With the acknowledgement of the boundaries that Bernice drew around her because of her inability to resolve the powerful internalized parental conflict came the freedom to seek new options.

The process of creating a living history theater play gave the group time to reflect and find a new structure, order and coherence in their lives that is so essential to self-definition, self-determination and empowerment in general. As members of Hodson Drama Group understood the social and historical circumstances that conditioned their life choices, they felt released to integrate past conflicts within themselves as black women living in an urban ghetto. For Bernice, in particular, the life review process helped her to develop a better understanding of her choices, come to a more accepting sense of herself, and build greater "ego integrity." The group liberated themselves by gaining a greater understanding of the nature of the heritage that bound their choices. Members identified significant personal, cultural and historical events. Thus, Bernice rediscovered the buried treasures of her past musical life. The gospel-jazz tradition became the metaphor which connected the players and the audience in a common celebration of a complex work history. As older women performers, they gave themselves permission to cross over generational history, bridging cultural conflicts in an act of self-determination. They were able to celebrate an integrated understanding of the continuity between past, present and hope for the future of black women in America. They became pioneers creating and performing the process of wrapping up and giving the gifts of their particular heritage.

SUMMARY AND CONCLUSIONS

In understanding the transmission of culture through living history theater, one can see the implications for social work with the elderly from psychosocial, programmatic, community and policy perspectives.

The cultural and historical perspective gained by enacting the work stories from the 1940s juxtaposed to the contemporary community scenes in the last act, provided the distance for compassion and appreciation of each person's particular circumstance within the black culture. Each member chose according to the opportunities they sought and found.

Only one generation ago, family and relatives lived within the same community. Old folks could easily tell stories to their grandchildren. Now there is a need to create a form for the passing on of the personal and historical legacy of the elders. Living history theater becomes an invention to consciously insure the continuity of culture. It becomes a definitional ceremony addressing the issue of cultural heritage, endowing each ethnic group with an opportunity to create new options for coping with social change. It becomes a tool to assist in the growth of self-determination for people engaged in the process of sharing stories.

The transmission of culture is a complex process. Through living history theater, each ethnic group has the opportunity to reflect and to comment on their heritage. In the process, the individual, group and community sift and sort through their cultural baggage, thus providing the lineage between past, present and future representations. In the process of creating a play, participants find their voice, tell survival stories and define their collective heritage. The audience bears witness to this accounting and validates their own experience. Life review is occurring for the individual, the group and the community.

The creating of the play becomes a therapeutic process in which older adults can dramatically represent developmental issues central to their psychosocial stage in the life cycle. Fundamental to the last stage is the need to cope with the crisis of continuous loss, culminating in death. In coping with death and dying, the facilitator addresses the task of life review: to help resolve past conflicts, to help find a form in which to leave a legacy. Integration through memory with earlier stages of being provides the sense of continuity and completeness that may be counted as an essential developmental task of old age.

In the group process, the elderly members create an identity based on shared past experiences and new adventures in theater and performance. They may also find ways of coping with isolation and depression. They often feel a sense of belonging and find a support network within the group. Programs based on life review can enhance the members' sense of self-esteem, sense of belonging and collective pride for a shared heritage. Some coping skills learned include respect for differences, mutual aid, and the formation of new friendships.

Living history theater can serve as a model for program development. All too often, group activities offered in senior centers, nursing homes and hospitals include bingo, low-level arts and crafts, sing-a longs, card playing and nonstop TV. These recreational programs do not directly address the psychosocial needs of the elderly. Programs should incorporate life review and relevant uses of the strengths of age—having lived a life.

Programs that address the need for continuity of culture and understand how ethnic survival depends on complex individuated patterns of behavior are vital to social work policy. Discontinuity of ethnic cultures means death to the rich heritage given to us from our native and immigrant past.

Commercial culture, with its freedom to obey the laws of the market, accountable only to the ledger sheet, acts regardless of the social consequences to the people affected. The country's cultural policy appropriates massive material resources for the expression of a dehumanizing and homogenizing mass culture. When a society creates homogenized images of ethnic groups, there is an implicit cultural policy of enforced forgetting of who we are and where we came from. Stereotyping ethnic groups inevitably leads to a denigration of the rich cultural diversity within each culture.

In contrast, the Hodson Living History Drama Group found a form to embrace its collective heritage. In the process of depicting their survival tale, they claimed their conflicts as their own, authenticating their voice and thereby empowering themselves and their respective community.

PRACTICE IMPLICATIONS

Many people are presently in the process of doing reminiscence work. There are resources available explaining and describing the particular life review projects in art, music, theater, writing, poetry and photography. Media projects include radio, video and film work. Intergenerational projects include different age groups working with both the frail and well elderly on a broad range of themes.

In developing programming, it is important to address the psychosocial needs of the elderly. Conscientious thought ought to be given to the values of shared learning, mutual respect and building on the strengths of people's life experiences. Life review activities can form the basis for developing meaningful programming for the elderly.

REFERENCES

Butler, Robert. *Why Survive? Being Old in America*. New York: Harper and Row, 1975.

Butler, Robert N. "The Life Review: An Interpretation of Reminiscence in the Aged." *Psychiatry*, Vol. 26, 1973, pp. 65-76.

Erikson, Eric. *Identity and the Life Cycle*. New York: International Universities Press, 1959.

Friere, Paolo. *Pedagogy of the Oppressed*. New York: Seabury Press, 1968.

Gelfand, Donald E. and Alfred J. Kitzik, eds. "Focuses and Issues." In *Ethnicity and Aging*. Vol. 5. New York: Springer Publishing Company, Inc., 1980, p. 2.

Glasser, P., R. Sam and R. Vinter, eds. *Individual Change Through Small Groups*. New York: The Free Press, 1974.

Hareven, Tamara. "The Search for Generational Memory: Tribal Rites in Industrial Society." *Daedalus*, 1975, pp. 137-148.

Holzberg. Carol S. "Ethnicity and Aging: Anthropological Perspectives on More Than Just the Minority Elderly." *Gerontologist*, Vol. 22, 1982, pp. 249-256.

Kirshenblatt-Gimblett, Barbara. "The Future of Folklore Studies in America: The Urban Frontier." *Folklore Forum*, Vol. 16, No. 2, 1983.

Myerhoff, Barbara and Simic, Andrei. *Life's Career-Aging: Cultural Variations in Growing Old*. California: Sage Publications, 1977.

Myerhoff, B. "Rites and Signs of Ripening: The Intertwining of Ritual, Time and Growing Older." In *Age and Anthropological Theory*. Ed. D. Kertier and J. Keith. Ithaca: Cornell University, pp. 305-329.

Myerhoff, B. "Telling One's Story." *The Center Magazine,* March 1980, pp. 22-40.

Myerhoff, B.G. *Number Our Days.* New York: E.P. Dutton, 1978.

Myerhoff, B.G. and V. Tufte. "Life History as Integration: An Essay on an Experimental Mode." *Gerontologist*, Vol. 15, No. 6, 1975, pp. 541-543.

Osgood, Nancy. "The Impact of Creative Dramatics on Black Elderly." Diss. Virginia Commonwealth University 1983.

Perlstein, Susan. *A State for Memory*. New York: Teachers and Writers Collaborative, 1981.

Perlstein, Susan. "Living History Theater." In *Uses of Reminiscence*. Ed. March Kaminsky. New York: The Haworth Press, 1984, pp. 37-51.

Sennett, Richard and Jonathan Cobb. *The Hidden Injuries of Class*. New York: Random House, 1972.

Spolin, Viola. *Improvisation for the Theater*. Illinois: Northwestern University Press, 1963.

Wallace, Michael. "The Politics of Public History." Past Meets Present Conference, New York, 8 Oct. 1984.

White, Robert. "Strategies of Adaptation: An Attempt at Systemic Description." In *Coping and Adaptation*. Ed. Coelho. New York: Basic Books, 1974.

Williams, Raymond. *The Sociology of Culture*. New York: Schocken Books, 1981.